How to Talk With Friends

A Step-by-Step Social Skills Curriculum for Children with Autism

Janine Toole PhD

First Printing, 2016

ISBN 978-0-9953208-02

Happy Frog Press

www.HappyFrogPress.com

About the Author

Janine Toole PhD

Dr Janine Toole is the founder of Happy Frog Press and Happy Frog Apps, creators of high-quality resources for elementary-aged children with autism and other social/language challenges.

Dr Toole's extensive experience in linguistics, software development and special needs learning underlies her firm belief that all children can learn – as long as we provide a learning environment that suits their needs.

www.Facebook.com/HappyFrogApps

@HappyFrogApps

www.HappyFrogApps.com

Table of Contents

Chapter 1
Introduction

Welcome to the *How to Talk with Friends* social skills curriculum!

This hands-on manual provides everything you need to run a successful social skills group or one-to-one intervention for children with Autism Spectrum Disorder (ASD), Asperger's or similar social skill deficits.

Making friends and maintaining friendships is a struggle for these learners. The *How to Talk with Friends* curriculum teaches ASD learners the key skills they need to talk and engage with their peers.

Students will learn how to:

- Begin a conversation by asking about their friend's interests.
- Respond to a friend with appropriate comments, follow-up questions and follow-up comments.
- Track the movement of a conversation topic and avoid getting stuck on his/her own special interest topic.
- Appropriately change a topic during a conversation without dropping it in like a bomb.
- Signal interest with eye contact and body orientation and also interpret a friend's face/body messages.
- Begin and end a conversation smoothly.

Children learn and practice these skills while playing games, doing crafts and hanging out with their friends. The focus is on extended practice to ensure mastery.

This manual is organized into two parts. Part 1 provides the background information you need to run a successful social skills group or one-to-one intervention. Individual chapters cover the course content and structure, course preparation, and course delivery and assessment.

Part 2 contains the twelve weekly lessons. Each lesson provides step-by-step instructions for pre-session preparation, session delivery and assessment, and parent communication. All materials for delivering the course are contained in the Appendices.

If you are new to this manual, we recommend you first read through all of Part 1 and the first three chapters of Part 2. After you have that basic understanding, you can use the manual as a reference to implement your successful social skills intervention.

Children with ASD can learn to engage with peers. This curriculum is the guide you need to ensure their success.

Curriculum Goals

The *How to Talk with Friends* social skills curriculum is designed for children with Autism Spectrum Disorder aged from 8 to 12 years old.

Children with ASD frequently demonstrate awkward or lagging social skills. In order to develop their skills, these children must learn and practice the skills in a structured environment. They then need support in generalizing these skills to the real world.

Social skills groups are a great environment for achieving these goals. Firstly, social skills groups are a structured environment where specific skills can be learned and practiced. Further, the presence of peers allows for generalization of these new skills to play situations like those found at home, on the playground and in the classroom.

In developing this group curriculum, we focused on the following goals.

Target 8 to12-year-olds

While there are many resources for younger children and some excellent materials for teenagers, there is little appropriate material for the tween age group.

Children in the tween age group talks with friends (like teens) but still plays games (like younger children). Materials for older or younger children are rarely appropriate for use with this group.

This curriculum targets 8 to 12-year-olds. However, it can also be adapted to younger or older audiences.

Build skills incrementally in small steps

Children with ASD need extensive practice with social skills in order to add them to their repertoire. The *How to Talk with Friends* curriculum focuses on small steps with lots of practice. We avoid the temptation to cover a large range of skills in shallow depth.

Instead, each week targets a specific skill that incrementally expands on the skills taught in previous weeks. Focusing on a specifically targeted skill allows for lots of practice. Moreover, expanding on previous skills allows these original skills to continue to be practiced week after week.

Focus on talking with friends

Tween children spend the majority of their time talking with people they know, mostly parents, teachers and friends. For this reason, the *How to Talk with Friends* curriculum focuses on the skills needed to talk appropriately with people they know.

This includes knowing what their friends are interested in, initiating and maintaining conversations about topics of shared interest, and beginning and ending a conversation.

Practice skills with real activities

Structured practice and role-play are excellent activities for learning a new skill. However, it is equally important that your ASD learners practice the social skills in as natural an environment as possible.

For that reason, during social group your learners will be engaged in active games, board games, and craft and building activities.

The *How to Talk with Friends* curriculum gradually steps the learners from structured practice to role-play to natural activities.

Design for a small group but provide adaptations for a one-to-one situation

It isn't always possible to find an appropriate peer for a social skills group, yet your ASD learner still needs to learn these skills. In this curriculum, we provide specific adaptations for a one-to-one situation.

Assume one coach, without specific training

Many social group curriculums assume you have a second adult available. Again, while this would be great, it is not always possible. Our curriculum assumes you have a single motivated adult who can lead the social skills group.

Similarly, often a parent or teacher knows a child needs social skills support but does not have specific training in social skills development or access to a trained individual. This manual does not assume any specific skills on the part of the trainer, apart from a motivation to help a child with ASD. Everything you need to know to get started is contained in these pages.

Provide generalization outside of class

In class, students will learn new skills and practice them during play. However, it is equally important that these skills are practiced out of class. The **How to Talk with Friends** curriculum provides specific homework for parents to complete with their child during the week.

This generalization step is key to student success.

Provide complete lesson guidance

If a curriculum is difficult to implement, it is likely that key components will be missed and learning will suffer. Our goal in developing this curriculum was to provide everything you need to deliver the curriculum.

The curriculum includes:

- **Weekly lesson plans** that include step-by-step instructions. Everything you need to do is described clearly. This includes pre-session preparation, lesson delivery, assessment and parent communication.
- **Scripted lessons.** All new learning material and role-play activities are scripted to make delivery even easier. You are, of course, free to use your own approach once you have identified the goal of each section.
- **All required content materials**. If you need a list of topics, they are provided in the lesson plan. If you need questions for a game show, they are provided. You can start a session with less than 5 minutes of preparation because all the content you need is provided. If you prefer independence, you are welcome to add your own materials.

- **Parent handouts**. Each week includes a parent handout with a lesson summary and a specific list of tasks that need to be completed.
- **Weekly assessment sheets**. Each weekly assessment sheet allows the quick gathering of data for post-session review.

These key criteria guided the development of the ***How to Talk with Friends*** curriculum. We also kept in mind best-practices for working with children with ASD, such as maintaining high levels of interest and engagement, targeting specific, measurable skills and providing appropriate rewards and motivation.

Chapter 2
Participants, Coaches & Parents

There are three key players in the journey to develop the social skills of a child with ASD. They are:

- The **coach** or teacher, who must have the skills and enthusiasm to take the learners on a fun but challenging journey to social skill success.
- The **students**(s), who must be ready to learn how to engage more successfully with their peers.
- The **parents**, who must take responsibility for out-of-class practice and generalization of the learned skills.

In this section, the roles and responsibilities of each of these key players are explained.

Coaches

Skills Required

This curriculum is ideal for use by speech pathologists, BCBA-accredited consultants and others trained to work with children with autism. The curriculum provides an evidence-based step-by-step development of key communication skills.

The curriculum is also suited to delivery by parents, behavior interventionists and education assistants. For this audience we include explicit instructions, all the required materials and detailed explanations for prompting, assessing and delivering the course.

No matter what your skills and experience, you can use this manual to run an effective and successful social skills group or one-to-one intervention.

For those less experienced, we have the following recommendations:

- Start with a smaller group of 2-3 students. This will allow you to build your skills and confidence in a simpler environment.
- Before conducting your first class, do a dry run of the entire session. This will give you much more confidence as you will identify gaps in your knowledge without the added pressure of having students in front of you.

In short, if you have a child in your life who needs to develop their social skills, dive in and help them. This manual will show you the way.

Additional Coaches

This curriculum is designed to be conducted by one coach with 1 to 4 students. This decision was driven by the reality that multiple skilled teachers are often either not available or not affordable.

If you have the luxury of an additional adult, you can increase the effectiveness of your class by:

- Increasing the number of students. We still recommend a maximum ratio of one adult to four learners.
- Using the additional adult to demonstrate the skills during the social topic lesson. This is especially useful if you have no neurotypical participants.
- Using the adult as additional eyes and ears to provide prompting during snack, practice sessions, games and other activities. This allows for more feedback per student and also allows the primary coach to complete the assessments more reliably.
- Having the additional adult answering parent questions at the beginning of the session while the primary coach gets the session started.

Participants

Group Composition & Size

The ideal size for a social group is 2 to 4 children. A maximum of four allows you to keep everyone engaged and active. Any larger and your ASD group members will frequently tune out.

It can be difficult to find appropriate group members, so we have also adapted this curriculum for use with one child. However, where possible, do your best to find a peer to join the group as your ASD student will progress more quickly.

Your group can contain a mix of ASD and neurotypical peers. Typical peers are a great resource for demonstrating the appropriate situational behavior. However, the curriculum is also effective if all your students have special needs.

All participants should meet the following basic criteria:

- Able to talk in sentences and answer questions on preferred topics.
- Able to attend in a small group setting without too many behavioral issues.

If the majority of requests to a child concern their behavioral choices, that child may not be a good choice for the group. Since only one adult coach is leading the group, the learning of all can get derailed if one individual constantly needs redirecting.

Our curriculum is directed at 8 to 12-year-olds. However, only small adaptations are needed for older or younger audiences.

Parents

Children with ASD learn best when lessons are reinforced and encouraged in multiple environments. In fact, this generalization is key to good progress.

For this reason, we give specific homework to parents. Most parents want to help their child as much as possible but aren't always sure what to do. The *How to Talk with Friends* curriculum provides parent letters that give explicit directions for what to do on a weekly basis.

We give parents the responsibility to ensure the homework is completed and ask them to hand in the worksheet weekly. Giving parents the responsibility increases the likelihood that the required tasks will be completed.

Chapter 3
Course Content & Structure

Skills Taught

Children in our targeted age range of 8 to 12 years need multiple skills in order to successfully interact with peers.

They first need the ability to engage in age-appropriate games. This includes active activities like hide-and-seek and tag. It also includes board games, computer games and the myriad of games that children invent on a daily basis.

Students also need to be able to talk, listen and respond to their friends in a meaningful way. Children with ASD are often adept at talking **AT** their friends - especially about their preferred topics. However, they often lack the ability to listen and respond meaningfully to what their friends say.

In the ***How to Talk with Friends*** curriculum, learners develop the skills of listening and responding appropriately to their friends. These skills are practiced in game-playing environments so that they can more easily generalize to real-life situations.

Each weekly lesson builds these skills incrementally. In the first week, students learn that other individuals have interests that differ from their own. They then learn how to identify shared interests - interests that two people have in common.

Students learn that most of our talk with a friend should be about shared interests.

The course then builds skills for successful conversations. For children with ASD, this requires teaching how to comment/respond and then continue a conversation, as well as how to appropriately change a topic.

The course also explicitly teaches how to notice cues with our eyes and ears to know if a person is interested, distracted, etc. The student also learns to make sure that their own body actions are conveying interest in the conversation and their friend.

The key to success with this curriculum lies in its narrow focus. Too often, children are taught a menu of different skills but don't get the chance to practice the skills and apply them in real situations.

In the *How to Talk with Friends* curriculum, the majority of time is spent practicing and generalizing the skills. This is vital for our ASD kids to integrate these skills into daily life.

Weekly Lesson Format

Each weekly lesson has a similar structure. This structure will quickly become familiar to your students, and the predictability will allow them to relax in the learning environment.

In describing the lesson format, we use a 2-hour weekly group session as our base timeframe. Later in this manual, you can find instructions to adjust for longer or shorter sessions.

The lesson guide provides suggested durations for each activity. However, don't be too constrained by these suggestions. If an activity is going well, let it continue for 5-10 minutes, though make sure you still leave your students wanting more. If an activity fails to engage your group, finish it early.

The only exception to this is the social skills topic. This section contains important information for your learners, and it should not be shortened or missed. It is also incredibly important to practice with role-play so your students really understand the lesson. This component should also be completed in full.

In the remainder of this section, we introduce the nine components of a social skills session. Each weekly lesson contains each of these components.

Preparation:

This section describes the tasks that the coach needs to complete before the group session. No other preparation is needed for the session beyond what is specified in this section.

Preparation may include:

- Room setup

- Snack preparation
- Printing any required worksheets, assessment sheets, etc.

Settle in Time: 5 minutes

The settle-in activity begins when the first student arrives. After greeting the student, the coach directs the child to the activity centers and asks them to play there until it is time for the group to start.

The settle-in activity allows students to tune into the group and space. Since the coach is not actively involved, it gives the coach the chance to greet students individually and answer any brief questions that parents may have. More involved questions should be gently deferred to after the social group.

Settle-in time should be limited to five minutes.

After Week 1, the settle-in time involves specific tasks for the coach as he/she greets the students. These tasks probe each student's skill at previously learned topics.

Group Activity: 5 minutes

The first activity is an active game with the whole group. The coach chooses a familiar activity that doesn't need much explanation. Tag or hide-and-seek work well.

Your students may have spent the day sitting in school. This activity will get them moving. It will also help establish that your group is a fun thing to do and not just work.

The extra time also allows late students to arrive without too much impact on their learning. In the case of late arrivals, greet the student and integrate them into the game. You should stay engaged with the game. For late arrivals, leave all parent discussion/questions until the end of the session.

During the 12 weeks of the course, switch the game that you choose for this activity. This encourages student flexibility. As well, it increases the range of games that your students can confidently play.

Social Skills Topic: 20 minutes

Each weekly lesson introduces a new social skill. During this section, the coach follows the lesson plan to present and demonstrate the topic. This is followed by guided role-play where each student gets a chance to practice the skill.

The social skill topic is scripted to make it easy for less experienced coaches. Key points about the scripts include:

- Explanations are short and concise because children with ASD typically are not great listeners.
- Explaining and questioning are constantly interspersed.

Interspersing explanations and questions has several benefits. The frequent need to retrieve information keeps students engaged and minimizes tuning out. The answers allow you to confirm understanding of the topic, and the repetition helps cement the information in the student's brain.

Be careful though, it is not YOUR repetition of the explanation that helps, it is the student repeatedly activating his own brain to retrieve an answer that aids learning. Make sure your students are constantly in action: thinking, answering and conversing.

Each social skill lesson also includes a role-play component. The role-play provides a highly supported environment to ensure students can demonstrate the new skill. This is a first step towards the more independent use of the skill that will develop during the remainder of the session.

Please keep in mind, it is very important that students be themselves and do not act different characters during role-play. Identifying our friend's interests and initiating conversations on shared interests is a key component of the *How to Talk with Friends* curriculum. It is impossible to develop this skill if each conversation involves a different character.

In the same manner, make sure students are honest about their interests and experiences. It is especially important for ASD students to learn that conversation is about **real** interests and events and is not a script that can be pulled from movies or TV shows they have watched.

Practice Activity: 10 Minutes

Immediately after the social skills lesson, students are assigned a structured activity that directly practices the skill just learned. This practice increases the likelihood that students will be able to demonstrate the skill during the more natural game-based activities in the remainder of the session.

Your role as a coach is to observe and prompt as needed in order to ensure student success.

Snack Break: 15 Minutes

During the snack break, the coach continues prompting new and previously learned social skills. Good social manners are also expected and prompted as needed.

Snack break serves several purposes:

- It provides a fun diversion after a period of learning and practicing new skills.
- It gives energy to children flagging from a long day at school.
- Snack and lunch breaks with peers are a daily occurrence for children in the school system. It is a key environment where social skills are needed.

Make sure you are aware of any allergies that your students may have.

Board Game Activity: 20 minutes

After snack, the group engages in a board game or similar activity. Instructions for the type of board games are given in the Required Materials section below.

Where possible, the decision of which game to play is delegated to the students. The coach prompts students through this process as needed, encouraging compromise and clear expression of preferences.

During the game, the coach is an observer, not a participant. He/she prompts for appropriate play, as needed. The coach also prompts use of the skills taught in this and previous lessons.

Game Show: 20 minutes

The game show segment is a fun activity that students enjoy.

The coach acts as a game show host, and the specific questions are provided in the weekly lesson plan. Like all other components of the social skills session, the game show directly practices and reinforces the skills taught in the current lesson.

A key part of the fun of the game show is having game show buzzers. These can be obtained online for about twenty dollars. The sillier the sounds, the better. More details can be found in the Required Materials section.

Final Group Activity: 15 minutes

In the last group component, the coach prompts the students to choose a final activity. In early weeks, the coach should give a choice of three for the students to discuss and decide.

In later weeks, when students become adept at deciding the group game, the coach may give more open-ended choices.

The suggestions provided by the coach may include board games, craft activities, building activities and active games. Keep in mind that the game should be a group or pair activity, where students are working towards a common goal and need to talk to each other.

Example of group craft and building activities include:

- The group builds a tower together, not individually.
- The group creates a craft robot together, not individually.
- Pairs of students build a Lego plane together.

Depending on how the session has gone, you may find you have no time for this final activity. That is fine. If other activities were continued because students were fully engaged with them, then you have met your goal of providing a structured, successful environment for learning and practicing new social skills.

On the other hand, you may find you have excess time remaining at the end of the session because earlier activities were not engaging for your group. That is also fine! There is no point continuing unsuccessful activities just to meet the schedule.

With extra time, extend this final activity. If necessary, switch activities part way through to keep students interested.

Parent Debrief: 10 minutes

If the previous activity was a building or craft activity, let the students continue while you debrief the parents. If the game was active or one which requires a high level of prompting, direct the students to the activity centers to play a game of their choice. Individual choices are acceptable at this time.

Each weekly lesson contains a parent letter. The parent letter explains the social skill introduced that week and assigns homework to the parent. Use this letter to structure your parent debrief.

Children with ASD need support in generalizing skills to new environments. The parent homework gives explicit instructions for generalization activities to be completed during the week. This step is key to your students' success.

We give responsibility for completing the homework to the parent as we want them to take an active role in ensuring the tasks are completed.

Parents hand in homework at the beginning of a session. If you notice over several sessions that a family is not completing the homework, have a private chat with them after the next session. Parents may not know the importance of generalization. Hopefully, with some gentle education and encouragement, they will get on board with supporting their child more actively.

Post Session

After students have left, complete the assessment sheet. Review each child's progress. Are there any skills that need more practice in next week's session?

Next, review the homework sheets handed in by the parents. Although completing homework is vital, there is no class time allocated for reviewing homework. This decision was made for several reasons:

- Class time is limited. Already you will find that you wished you had more time to practice the targeted skills.
- Reviewing homework is not practicing social skills. In your class time, you want to spend the maximum time possible teaching and practicing social skills. Anything that deviates from that reduces your students' learning possibilities.

While reviewing the homework sheets, consider how each student is doing and how you may need to adjust your level of prompting next week.

Any concerns with how the homework is being completed should be addressed specifically with the parent after the group parent debrief.

Session Length

The lesson plans in this manual are designed for a weekly 2-hour social group. A two-hour session allows for learning, practice, fun and snack. The length works well for 8 to 12-year-olds.

However, the curriculum is easily adapted to longer or shorter sessions. See below for specific recommendations.

Longer Sessions

If you choose to do a longer session, intersperse the prescribed activities with 10 to 15-minute sessions of free play. Children with ASD often need alone-time to recharge. The free play will allow them to be ready to learn when needed during the longer time period.

With extra time, you can also include another group activity, following the instructions found in each weekly lesson.

90 Minute Session

If you only have ninety minutes, remove one game session, reduce the snack and make some activities briefer. Depending on the time of day and the age of your students, you may choose to remove snack. Though keep in mind that eating together is a real-world activity that children engage in frequently. It is a great time to practice social skills.

A sample schedule for a 90-minute session.

> 0- 5: Arrivals and greetings
>
> 5- 10: Warmup activity
>
> 10-30: Social topic and role-play
>
> 30-40: Practice activity
>
> 40-50: Snack
>
> 50-65: Board game
>
> 65-80: Game show
>
> 80-90: Parent debrief

60 Minute Session

If you only have 60 minutes per session, you have two options. The first (and preferred) option is to follow the 2-hour schedule and split it over 2 sessions. This option allows for adequate practice of each skill. This repetition is vital for ASD learners.

Week 1	Week 2
0-5: Arrival & greetings	0-5: Arrival & greetings
5-25: Social topic & role-play	5-15: Social topic review
25-35: Practice activity	15–35: Game show
35-50: Board game	35-50: Group Activity
50-60: Parent debrief	50-60: Parent debrief

An alternative option is to reduce the week's activities. Skip the Warmup Activity (5 minutes), Snack (10 minutes) and Board Game (15 minutes). That leaves you with a session that looks like this.

> 0-5: Arrival & greetings
>
> 5-25: Social topic & role-play
>
> 25-35: Practice activity
>
> 35-50: Board game/Game show*
>
> 50-60: Parent debrief

* In the 60-minute schedule, alternate the game show and board game activities each week.

30 Minute Sessions

If you have only 30 minutes per session, we encourage you to have multiple sessions per week. Social skills do not come easily to children with ASD so frequent practice is needed.

For a 30-minute session, we recommend you choose one main activity from the standard session and bracket it with intro and exit activities. Here is a sample 5-day schedule to cover a standard 2-hour session in one week.

Monday

0-5: Arrival & greetings

5-25: Social skills topic & brief role-play

25-30: Summarize & debrief

Tuesday

0-5: Arrival & greetings

5-10: Topic recap

10-25: Role-play & practice activity

25-30: Summarize & debrief

Wednesday

0-5: Arrivals & greetings

5-10: Topic recap

10-25: Board game

25-30: Summarize & debrief

Thursday

0-5: Arrivals & greetings

5-10: Topic recap

10-25: Game show

25-30: Summarize & debrief

Friday

0-5: Arrivals & greetings

5-10: Topic recap

10-25: Group activity

25-30: Summarize & debrief

Homework sheets can be given to parents on Wednesday for return the following Tuesday.

Teaching One-to-One

In an ideal world, peers would always be available for an ASD-oriented social group. However, in reality, there are cases where a child desperately needs social skills development, but an appropriate peer is not available.

If this is your situation, just get started with what you have. If an appropriate peer becomes available, restart the curriculum at the beginning. There is absolutely no disadvantage to this. Your student will benefit greatly from the additional practice and generalization.

Here's how to adapt the lessons to a situation with one adult and one child.

Role Switch Between Coach and Participant

During the lesson, you will often need to switch from coach to participant, and back again. To make this successful, integrate the following suggestions:

- Identify a teacher location and a participant location.

When you are the teacher, stand in the teacher location. Next to the whiteboard is a good location.

When you are a participant, move to a position away from your teacher location.

This approach isn't ideal as you will need to prompt while in the participant role. However, it does at least attempt to differentiate the two different roles you will play.

- Use non-verbal prompts while acting as participant

Rely on gestures and visual prompts when you need to act as the coach while in the participant role. Since you will be talking in your role as a participant, using non-verbal prompts and gestures will minimize the disruption to the conversation.

Pointing at the board and having ready-made signs can help in this regard.

   - Be yourself

When you switch into the participant role, make sure you remain yourself and don't role-play being someone else. During the course, students learn each other's interests and initiate conversation based on shared interests. If you become someone else in different conversations, students will be unable to develop these key skills.

Also, as mentioned previously, ASD students must learn that conversation is about **real** interests and events. If you role-play different interests and personalities from one conversation to the next, your students will too.

Be prepared for activities to move faster

With only one student, you will find that activities will take less time.

You might find that you can complete the 2-hour session in 90 minutes. This is fine. Don't prolong activities just to fit the schedule.

Chapter 4
Preparing for the Course

In this chapter, we discuss the preparations necessary to deliver the social skills curriculum as either a social group or one-to-one intervention. This includes:

- Group location
- Required materials
- Downloadable resources

Group Location

Any space can work for a social group: a home, classroom, etc. All your required materials are portable so you can set up your group anywhere.

You will need an area where you can set up your whiteboard, with seats so that everyone can see the board and each other. In another area (same room or different), set up your stations: craft station, building station and board game station. In each location, there should be enough space for all children to participate in the activity.

Our social group curriculum also includes active games like tag and hide-and-seek. Do the best you can with the space you have available. If you are working at the home of one of the parents, request permission for using a rec room for more rambunctious games. Depending on the weather and location, playing outside may be a good alternative.

If you only have a small space, modify the games so they work. For example, with tag, you can require that everyone has to move like a penguin or walk on their knees. The main goal is to get them moving, active in the game and focused on each other.

Required Materials

To successfully run the social group, you should have the following materials available.

Whiteboard

A whiteboard (2' x 3' minimum) is invaluable during the learning part of the session. The coach can jot down the children's ideas during brainstorming, summarize instructions for those with working memory issues, etc. A large sketch pad can easily substitute.

3 Or More Board Games

You will need at least 3 age-appropriate board games. Make sure the games are suitable for the cognitive age of your group. Choose games that are super-fun and move quickly. The game should finish within 10-15 minutes. Your students may not have the stamina for long drawn-out games.

Games we recommend are Cadoo, Headbanz and Labyrinth Junior. Parents may also have suggestions for games that their child enjoys.

During the 12-week course, update your selection with new games. This expands students' skills and keeps them interested. If a game is played but is unsuccessful with your group, feel free to switch it out immediately.

Craft Station

You will need a collection of craft materials that intrigue your students. You can buy kits online or make your own with a visit to a stationery store.

It is good to have a few items in the craft kit that are new, unique or intriguing in some way. Where possible, make these items only available during social group.

Building Materials

You will need some building materials like Lego or Kapla blocks. You don't need a huge amount. Just enough for each of your students to build something small without running out of blocks.

Game Show Buzzers

Each week, learners participate in a game show activity. Having silly buzzers keeps the fun level high. Even though these are not mandatory, we strongly recommend them.

These can be purchased online for about twenty dollars.

A List of Active Games

All children need to blow off energy, especially if they are working hard. Have a set of go-to active games like tag or hide-and-seek. Use tried-and-true favorites, but also mix it up occasionally to keep things fresh.

Downloadable Materials

For ease of printing, the parent handouts and assessment pages are available on our website in a handy PDF.

Please go to www.happyfrogapps.com/talking-friends-download

Keeping References Current

Throughout this course we refer to specific movies, apps and activities. These may not be relevant to your students. Feel free to replace any suggestion of an app, game or movie with something more current.

Chapter 5
Delivering & Assessing the Course

In the previous chapter, we covered the requirements for setting up the social skills group. This chapter covers the issues you need to consider as you deliver the course.

The topics include:

- Prompting
- Error correction
- Progression
- Assessment
- Motivation & rewards

Prompting

Students improve when they practice what they should say rather than get more practice at what they shouldn't say. The purpose of a prompt is to guide a student toward a correct answer and avoid an incorrect answer.

Prompts can be verbal, visual or gestural. Successful prompting increases the amount of correct answers and reduces the number of incorrect answers.

Types of Prompts

There are many different types of prompts, but the types you will most often use when teaching social skills are gestures, visual prompts, and partial or full verbal prompts.

Gestures

A gestural prompt is a physical movement that provides a clue to the student about what behavior is required.

The gesture can be something universal like a point. Alternatively, you can develop specific gestures to indicate a specific suggestion. For example, with my students I often use a circular motion with my finger. My students learn that this means keep going.

Restrict your invention of novel gestures to one or two. You don't want your student to struggle to remember what your gesture means. This can happen if you have too many.

Gestures are great because they are the least intrusive prompt. If a prompt is needed, where possible, start with a gestural prompt.

Visual Prompts

A visual prompt directs a student's attention to visual information in the environment as a clue to what behavior is required. For example, you can point to a rule or diagram on a whiteboard. You can hold up a sign that has a clue word or image.

Visual prompts are great because they do not interrupt a conversation with additional words. Students can reference the prompt while still maintaining their engagement with a peer.

Visual prompts are less obtrusive than verbal prompts but more intrusive than gestural prompts. Use when gestural prompts do not promote the required behavior.

Partial or Full Verbal Prompts

Verbal prompts are spoken words that suggest the required student behavior.

Where possible, limit your prompt to a partial verbal prompt and use a full verbal prompt only when absolutely required.

A partial verbal prompt provides a brief clue or a partial response that the student can copy.

A full verbal prompt provides a full response that the student can copy. A full verbal prompt is NOT explanatory in any way. It is simply a sample answer that the student can immediately copy to continue the peer interaction.

For example, if student Lisa is having trouble asking student John about his interests, some full and partial prompts to Lisa could be:

> Coach: "John, what did you do...." *(partial verbal prompt giving partial response)*

Coach: "Lisa, think about weekend activities..." (partial verbal prompt giving a clue)

Coach: "John, what did you do on the weekend?" (full verbal prompt giving full response)

Avoid Prompt Dependence

Students can learn to reply on prompts. In this situation, they will wait for you to prompt to make answering easier for them.

In order to avoid this dependence, fade prompts as quickly as possible. Fading prompts means moving from your current prompt to a less intrusive prompt. If you are using a full verbal prompt, try using a partial verbal prompt. If you are using a partial verbal prompt, move to a visual or gestural prompt. Next step would be to use no prompt and simply wait for your student to answer.

Waiting is difficult, and many instructors jump in with a prompt after a second or two of silence. This is too quick. During this course your students are learning difficult skills and it may take a few moments for them to consider who they are talking to, recall an appropriate interest and then formulate a question. While we want this skill to become fluent eventually, allow your student enough time to think it through. Don't immediately jump in with a prompt.

When to Use Prompts

Use a prompt when your student:

- Is about to give an incorrect response.
- Gives an incorrect response.
- Doesn't begin to respond after 5 seconds. (Count to 5 slowly)

Remember, where possible we want to avoid our students getting practice at incorrect responses. We want all practice to be correct responses. Use appropriate prompts to make this happen.

Correcting Errors

Even with excellent prompting skills, your students will still make errors. We suggest a 3-step approach to error correction.

1. Identify a positive aspect of the student's response.
2. Identify the problem.

3. Prompt for a correct answer.

For example, if a student asks a follow-up question that is not related to the topic of conversation, you could respond as follows:

> *Joe, that was an interesting question. But it wasn't related to the topic of eating dinner. Can you think of a different question that is related to the topic of eating dinner?*

If you know your student needs more support, try a partial verbal prompt. For example:

> *Joe, that was an interesting question, but it wasn't related to the topic of eating dinner. How about something like, what did YOU have...? (Include a gestural prompt for the student to continue.)*

Assessment

Each weekly lesson has an assessment sheet targeted to the skills taught in that lesson. Only one copy is needed for up to four students.

The assessment allows you to see how students perform on the task introduced that week. At the end of the session, use the assessment to identify students who may need a little extra support in the following weeks.

At the end of the course, you can use these assessments to write up progress summaries for your students.

The assessments are designed for the coach's use and not for distribution to parents.

For many of the activities during the session, the assessment sheet specifies a target behavior. After the activity, the coach scores each student as follows:

++ Mostly without prompting

Use this code if your student performs the required task without prompting, or occasionally needs a gestural or visual prompt.

✚ Mostly with minor prompting

Use this code if your student often needs gestural or visual prompts and occasionally needs full or partial verbal prompts.

➖ Mostly with extensive prompting

Use this code if your student often needs partial or full verbal prompts.

N/A

Use this code if the student did not have the opportunity to achieve the specified task during the activity.

Progression

This course consists of twelve weekly lessons. Each skill builds on the previous skills, so it is important to go in order from week 1 to week 12.

However, don't be afraid to repeat a week or two if your students are not demonstrating independent use of the skill in structured activities. It is better to cover less material if your students need extra practice.

Your weekly assessment sheets, your experience in class and the completed parent homework will provide the data you need to make an appropriate decision.

Halfway through the course, there is an explicit checkpoint for you to evaluate whether some lessons should be repeated. Further information is given at the end of Week 6. In Appendix A, you can find a parent handout that directly addresses this issue if you decide repetition is necessary.

Motivation & Rewards

Learning and practicing social skills is hard work for children with ASD. You may need to provide additional motivation for your students to participate fully.

Children with ASD can be motivated in many ways. We suggest the following:

Enthusiasm and Fast Pace

If you bring enthusiasm, a fast pace and a fun-filled attitude, you may engender all the motivation you need from your students. Children love to feel successful, so make your session exciting, fast paced and full of praise.

If you can keep your students engaged with your enthusiasm, you will teach them a lot about the benefits and rewards of social engagement.

Token Systems

Your group may need external motivation to actively engage with each other. In this case, a token system could be a good choice. Token systems are an effective method for children who are not intrinsically motivated to participate.

A token system is a system for providing positive reinforcement by giving tokens immediately after specific behaviors are demonstrated. At a later time, the tokens are exchanged for prearranged rewards. The child is motivated to perform the desired behavior in order to earn the desired reward.

The tokens are a reward for demonstrated behavior, not a bribe for future behavior. Research shows that effective use of a token system increases the frequency of the targeted behavior.

There are many ways to implement a token system. A quick web search can give you lots of ideas. In terms of the issues to consider, Miltenberger (*Behavior Modification* 2008. Belmont California, Wadsworth Publishing, p.498) lists seven components that need to be defined when implementing a token system. These are:

> - The desirable target behaviors to be strengthened.
> - The tokens to be used as reinforcers.
> - A list of rewards to be exchanged for tokens.
> - A reinforcement schedule for token delivery.
> - The cost in tokens for each reward.
> - The time and place for exchanging tokens for rewards.
> - Whether there will be a response cost component, where tokens are lost for specific undesirable behaviors.

You should also consider whether your students will earn tokens as a group, or individually.

A token system can make a powerful difference if your students are not inherently motivated to participate actively in the group.

Is this book helpful so far?

If so, please leave a review on Amazon. It makes a huge difference to us!

You don't need to purchase the book on Amazon to leave a review.

Go to your local Amazon website and search for 'social skills curriculum'. Select this book and down near the reviews you will see an 'Add a Review' button.

Part 2

Introduction

In Part 1 we provided the background information you need to run a social skills group for learners with ASD. In Part 2, you will find a step-by-step guide for each of the twelve weekly lessons.

If you are new to the **How to Talk with Friends** curriculum, browse through the first three lessons to get a feel for the structure and content of the lessons.

You will notice that scripted elements are contained in boxes. For example:

> *Hey everyone, welcome to our social group. We are going to have a fun time and learn some useful skills. Right now, we are going to have 15 minutes at the sitting area. After that, we will play some more games.*

Specific actions that you need to perform are designated with an arrow. For example:

» Write the following rule on the board: We talk to friends about shared interests.

Throughout the lesson plans, we assume a social skills group consisting of four 8 to 12-year-old learners: Joe, Lisa, Kelly and Peter.

Week 1 Discovering Shared Interests

Background

The first week focuses on identifying the interests of each group member and helping each member identify the interests he shares with the other group members.

It is important to know about shared interests because most conversations focus on shared interests. ASD students in your group most likely talk about their own special interests instead of shared interests. This lesson is the first step in helping them to think about other people's interests.

Before learners can talk about common interests, they need to know how to discover someone else's interests. The Week 1 lesson teaches this skill and gives the students many opportunities to practice.

Lesson Content

Preparation:

> » Set up your space to suit your needs. Ideally, you will have a sitting area, a centers area and an active area. Identify an area where you want parents to wait at the end of the session.
> » In your centers area, set up craft, building and board game stations.
> » Divide your whiteboard into 3 sections. In the top section, divide the area into four boxes. Put each student's name at the top of a box.

» Print out one Detective Notes page for each child. Prepare the detective notes by putting the student name in the first box and the other students' names in the appropriate boxes. Detective Notes are found in Appendix A.

» Print out the Week 1 assessment sheet. Please see Appendix C.

» Print out the parent debrief notes for yourself and one parent handout for each child. Please see Appendix B.

» Make sure you have a snack ready to serve, but keep it out of view until snack time.

Settle in: 5 Minutes

As students arrive, greet them enthusiastically and then direct them to the centers area, letting them know they will have five minutes to play before the group starts.

Let the parents know what time to return and where to wait. Explain that you will give them a debriefing at the end of the session. Where possible save questions for the debrief.

Warm up Activity: 5 minutes

After all the students have arrived, gather them quickly into a fun active game. Keep instructions to a minimum by choosing a game that most children are familiar with. Tag is a good choice because it is well-known and fun and you can get started quickly.

As you play, use your students' names so that the children became familiar with their peers.

> *Good catch, Joe.*
>
> *You're really fast, Kelly.*
>
> *Peter, get Lisa!*

Social Skills Topic: 20 minutes

After no more than five minutes of the active game, direct everyone to the seating area. Welcome them and set expectations for the next 15 minutes. ASD learners typically don't have great skills at attending and listening, so keep information to a minimum.

Hey everyone, welcome to our social group. We are going to have a fun time and learn some useful skills. Right now, we have 15 minutes at the sitting area. After that, we will play some more games.

As you review the script in this section, note the frequent use of questions. These questions confirm understanding, and the repetition helps cement the information in the student's brain. Be careful though, it is not YOUR repetition that helps, it is the student repeatedly activating his own brain that aids learning.

Make sure your students are constantly in action: thinking, answering and conversing.

1.1 Identify interests

In the first activity, you identify one or more interests for each child. This exercise is also a chance to introduce everyone's names.

Today we are going to learn about shared interests. A shared interest is something two people like. Let's see what shared interests we can find in this group.

Everyone, this is Peter. Peter, what is your favorite video game?

» Write Peter's answer on the whiteboard under his name. (In the top section that you prepared before class). Then check to see if anyone else has that same interest.

Awesome, I like Minecraft, too. Does anyone else like Minecraft?

» If anyone answers in the affirmative, put the same interest under their name. Now move on to the next student.

Kelly, what is your favorite sport?

» Write Kelly's answer under her name.

> *Soccer is great. Does anyone else like soccer?*

Continue on, asking each student one question and then checking if other students have the same interest. Any time a student identifies an interest, note it under their name.

Stop after each student has been introduced and has provided an answer. Move quickly without bogging down into a discussion of each topic. If a student is talkative, you can gently explain that you already have three interests noted down for him, so you don't need any more right now.

Some questions you can use are:

> *What's your favorite movie?*
>
> *What fun thing did you do last weekend?*
>
> *What's your favorite thing to eat?*
>
> *If you had five dollars, what would you spend it on?*

Make sure you have at least 2-3 **common** interests identified on the board i.e. the same interest listed under more than one student. If need be, at the end, ask a question like, "Who likes computer games?" or "Who likes pizza?"

1.2 Identify shared interests

In the next step, you help students identify interests that they have in common with other students. You also introduce the idea that shared interests make good conversation topics. Again, move quickly.

» Point at the board.

> *Now, this is interesting, I see some common interests. Remember, a common interest*
>
> *is when you and someone else both like the same thing. We say you have a common*
>
> *interest or a shared interest.*

Can anyone see any common interests?

» Give your students at least 10 seconds to look at the board, Then, if needed, point to an interest that is listed under more than one student.

Look, I see that Joe likes Minecraft. Does anyone else here have Minecraft next to their name?

» Wait for the students to respond.

Yes, you're right. Lisa and Joe both like Minecraft. They have a common interest.

Do you think Joe likes talking about Minecraft?

» Wait for students to respond.

Do you think Lisa likes talking about Minecraft?

» Wait for students to respond.

So, what should Joe and Lisa talk about to each other?

» Students respond.

Yes! Both Joe and Lisa like Minecraft, so they should talk about Minecraft with each other. Joe, would you enjoy that?

» Wait for Joe to respond.

Lisa, would you enjoy that?

» Wait for Lisa to respond.

Yes, everyone has fun if you are talking about common interests.

Now, I have a friend Liam who does NOT like Minecraft. Uh-uh. He really hates it. Should I talk to him about Minecraft?

» Wait for students to respond.

Why shouldn't I talk to him about Minecraft?

» Wait for students to respond.

Right! He's not interested in Minecraft, so I shouldn't talk to him about Minecraft.

Let's make a rule about this and write it up on the board. When we talk with a friend, we should talk about...?

» Wait for students to respond.

» Write in the middle section of the whiteboard, in big letters: Talk to friends about shared interests.

1.3 Teach Get-to-know-you question: What is your favorite___?

In the next two sections, you teach your students two easy question types that they can use to discover common interests. Students practice using these questions to find out the interests of other students. The first question to teach is the 'what is your favorite___?' question.

Now, what if you haven't really been paying attention, and you are not sure what your friend is interested in?

No problem! I'm going to teach you two easy question types that will help you discover what your friend is interested in. We'll call these Get-to-know-you questions.

» Write **Get to Know You Questions** on the whiteboard in the bottom section.

The first question type is this:

What is your favorite _____ ?

» Write the question on the whiteboard in the bottom section and read it aloud.

Now, I could ask: What is your favorite video game? What is your favorite movie? What other favorite questions could I ask?

» Wait for several student responses. Repeat each and praise. If error, adapt and praise.

*Yes, 'what is your favorite sport?' Excellent. Joe, can you think of a **favorite** question?*

Next, you will do role-plays where the students get a chance to ask and answer **favorite** questions. Request a student to stand up and ask you a **favorite** question. Answer and reciprocate.

Student: What is your favorite sport?

You: My favorite sport is baseball. The New York Yankees are my favorite team. What's your favorite sport?

Student responds.

Next, select students in pairs to stand up and role-play. The question must be different every time, so leave your more skilled students until the end. Each student should get a chance to ask a 'favorite' question.

Before you move on to the second question type, remind students why the *favorite* question is useful.

> *Fantastic! You guys are great at asking and answering favorite questions. Now, can someone remind me why we might ask a **favorite** question?*

» Wait for student response.

> *Yes, that's right! We can use a **favorite** question to find out what our friends are interested in. That helps us figure out our shared interests!*
>
> *Why is it good to know what our shared interests are?*

» Wait for student response.

> *Yes. Shared interests or common interests are topics that we are both interested in, so they are good things to talk about! We don't want to talk about something that our friend is NOT interested in. So we need to know what they ARE interested in.*

1.4 Teach Get-to-know-you question: What did you do last___?

After your students have practiced the first question type, you now teach them the second question type. This is the 'what did you do last ___?' question. Both of these questions help students identify their friend's interests.

Now, I'm going to teach you another question type that is awesome for discovering what our friends are interested in. Here it is.

» Write the following question on the board and say it aloud.

What did you do last weekend?

Demonstrate how this question can help you discover what your friends are interested in.

Lisa, ask me this question.

» Lisa asks: What did you do on the weekend?

I had a fantastic weekend. I went camping on Galiano Island and I went fishing!

So, Lisa, can you name one thing I am interested in?

» Lisa responds with camping or fishing.

Yes, I like camping. Peter, can you guess another one of my interests?

» Peter responds.

Yes. I love fishing too! By asking this question, you found out two of my interests. Nice job!

You can mix this question up a bit, too. If you see your friend after summer vacation, you could ask... What did you do...?

» Wait for student response.

> *Yes. What did you do during the summer? Or, if it is Friday, you could find out your friend's plans for the weekend by asking...*

» Wait for student response.

> *Yes. What are you doing this weekend? Awesome. Let's practice that.*

Pick two students to role-play. Make sure the question is reciprocated before the role-play is complete.

Continue with role-play practice until each student has a chance to ask the question. It is great if they ask a unique what-are-you-doing question, but it is okay if they revert to the standard "What did you do on the weekend?" question.

Congratulate everyone, then quickly summarize the information they have learned.

> *Great job everyone. Now, just remind me. Why might we ask about someone's weekend activities?*

» Wait for student response.

> *Yes. We could ask that question to find out what they are interested in and what they like to do. Why do we want to know what they are interested in?*

» Wait for student response.

> *Yes! So we know what to talk about. Because our rule is...?*

» Point to the rule so students can read it aloud.

» Wait for student response.

> *Awesome. When we talk to friends, we need to talk about things we are BOTH*
>
> *interested in. Great job everyone! We are done here, and now we get to play a game!*

Detective Activity: 10 minutes

In this activity, students use questions to find out their friend's interests. Their goal is to find at least one common interest with each student. Leave the whiteboard in view so the students can look at it to remind themselves of the questions they can use.

This activity is an important step towards getting students to demonstrate the skill during the more natural game-based activities in the remainder of the session.

> *Okay, everyone, stand up and come over here. We are going to play a detective game*
>
> *and discover some common interests. I am going to give each of you a sheet of paper*
>
> *which has your name at the top and everyone else's name in a box on the page.*
>
> *Your job is to ask each other questions and find at least 3 interests for each person.*
>
> *Write those interests in the box with their name on it.*
>
> *If it is a shared interest, you should put a circle around it. So, if Kelly is interested in*
>
> *baking and you are too, put a circle around it.*
>
> *So how many interests for each person?*

» Wait for student response.

> *Yes, at least 3 interests for each person. And what do you do if you find a common*
>
> *interest?*

» Wait for student response.

Yes, you put a circle around it. And what are the two types of questions that you can use?

» Wait for student response. Point to the board if necessary.

*Yes. You can use a **favorite** question, like "What is your favorite movie?" What other type of question can you use?*

» Wait for student response.

Yes. You can ask what they did on the weekend. I'd like you to use each of those questions while you are looking for common interests. Okay? Both types of questions.

If you are confused and need help, who do you ask?

» Wait for student response.

Yes, just ask me! Right. Here are your detective notes and a pencil. We will take about 10 minutes to do this.

Watch as the students commence the task. Once things are underway, grab your weekly assessment sheet and complete the section for this activity.

The assessment evaluates whether each student uses the two sentence types while getting the information about their partner's interests.

At any point, if you identify someone who needs a little more support, step in with an appropriate level of prompting. Assessment is important, but it is more important to provide prompting when it is needed to learn a new skill.

Make sure to stay in an observer role and do not participate.

When there are only a few minutes left, do a quick review by asking questions like the following:

Lisa, can you tell me something that Kelly is interested in?

Peter, what common interest do you have with Joe?

» At the end, praise the students and retrieve the detective notes.

Great job, everyone! Our time is up so please pass your sheets to me. We'll use them again later. You'll be pleased to know our next activity is snack!

Snack Break: 15 minutes

Get snack started. Then briefly mark the assessment sheet for the previous activity if you have not completed it.

During the snack break, refer to the detective notes to suggest particular topics of conversation. Do this informally. Your goal is to prompt conversation between the students and not to be part of the conversation yourself.

Hey Joe, you and Kelly both like baking. What question could you ask her about that?

If you have a moment, fill in the assessment sheet for snack.

Board Game Activity: 20 minutes

Have a selection of 3 board games available. Fast-moving games that take only 10-15 minutes to play are best. Students should have fun while they play.

Ask your students to decide amongst themselves which game to play. The decision should take less than a minute. Prompt as needed to help the children develop the skill of making a group decision.

Get the game started, explaining as needed to those unfamiliar with the game. Depending on the skill level of your students, you could request another student to explain the game if they are familiar with it.

Only the students play the game. During the game, your job is to monitor and prompt good game behavior - taking turns, being fair, being supportive, etc.

If possible, also encourage conversation in the same way as you did during snack, by identifying a specific common interest that two students have.

Towards the end, fill in the assessment sheet for this activity. You will note the level of support the student needed to play the game: no support, some support, or lots of support. You will also note if each student initiated conversation based on your explicit prompt or if they initiated conversation without prompting.

If the game is going well, continue it without comment. If the game is not successful, finish it early.

> *Hey, we have run out of time for this today. Let's pack up and get on to our next activity. I think you'll love it!*

Game Show: 20 minutes

Practicing social skills is hard work for children with ASD, so your students are probably getting tired. This next activity is fun and high energy and will recharge your students. If you have silly buzzers, your learners are guaranteed to have a good time. The activity reinforces the common interests that students have previously identified.

> *For our next activity, we are going to play a game show. You are the contestants, and I am the announcer. We have these awesome buzzers.*

» Hand out the buzzers.

> *Everyone, try out your buzzer. Cool, huh? You will also need your detective notes in order to answer correctly.*

» Hand out the detective notes from the detective activity.

All right. Get ready to listen to the first question. If you know the answer, press your buzzer. If you yell out the answer, your answer doesn't count. So what do you need to do if you know the answer?

» Wait for student response.

Yes. You press the buzzer. Okay, here is the first question. What is something Peter is interested in?

» Wait for student response.

Ask the first person to buzz for their answer. If incorrect, move on to another student.

Ask variants of the following questions.

Tell me something that _____ is interested in.

Which student is interested in _____?

Which two students share an interest in _____?

Which student is NOT interested in _____?

Who would you talk to about_____?

What is a good topic for when you are talking to _____?

While the students are having fun, keep the game going. As the game winds down, finish up the activity.

Fantastic job, everyone! You have learned a lot about the things your friends are interested in. Now, tell me again, why do we want to know what our friends are interested in?

» Wait for student response.

> *Yes. So you know what to talk about. Because our rule is to talk about shared interests.*

» Collect the detective notes and move on to the next activity.

Group Activity: 15 minutes

Identify whether you want your students to do a board game, active game, craft or building activity. Your choice will depend on the energy level and current behavior of your students.

Once you have identified the type of game, give your students a choice of 3 options and get them to decide between them what they want to do.

Get the activity started, explaining as needed to those unfamiliar with the activity. Depending on the skill level of your students, you could request another student to explain.

Only the students engage in the activity. Your job is to monitor and prompt good game behavior - taking turns, being fair, being supportive, etc.

If possible, also encourage conversation by identifying a specific common interest that two students have.

If you have a moment, complete the assessment for the game show activity. You will note the level of participation and the success at answering the questions.

Towards the end, fill in the assessment sheet for this activity. You will note the level of support the student needed for the activity: no support, some support or lots of support. You will also note if each student successfully initiated conversation based on your explicit prompt or if they initiated conversation without prompting.

As parents start to arrive, finish up the activity, unless it is one the students can continue without support.

> *Okay, let's pack up this game. Once we are done, I'd like you to go over to the centers area. You will find craft materials and building blocks. Choose anything you'd like to do while I tell your parents how awesomely you did today.*

Parent Debrief: 10 minutes

The purpose of the parent debrief is to educate the parents about the specific skills taught in this lesson, introduce the homework assignment and answer any questions they may have.

Refer to the parent debrief notes in Appendix A for the course-related details you should cover in the first week's debrief. Use the Week 1 homework sheet to introduce this week's homework.

Post Session

Take 5 minutes to review your assessment, adding any extra data or notes that you couldn't include during the session. Consider the following question for each student:

> Did this student successfully ask a question to identify an interest during the group activities?

Overall, ask yourself whether the students are ready to move on to Week 2, or if it would be best to provide another week of practice at this skill. See the section on Progression in Part 1 of this manual for background to make your decision.

Week 2
Topic-starter
Questions

Background

This week students learn how to ask **topic-starter questions**. A topic-starter question can be used to start a conversation with a friend or begin a new topic during a conversation. Students use information about shared interests to ask appropriate topic-starter questions.

Students will learn that topic-starter questions:

- Should be about their friend's interests.
- Should be about recent events or activities.

Lesson Content

Preparation:

» Set up your space to suit your needs. Ideally, you will have a sitting area, a centers area and an active area.
» In your centers area, set up craft, building and board game stations.
» Have the students' detective notes from last week available. Review the sheets so you can recall at least one interest for each student.

» Review the game show questions for Week 2 in Appendix B. Print if preferred.
» Print a copy of the Week 2 assessment sheet as well as a parent handout for each child.
» Make sure you have a snack ready to serve, but keep it out of view until snack time.

Settle in: 5 Minutes

As students arrive, greet them and ask each a question related to one of their interests.

> *Hey, Peter. Did you play Minecraft this week?*

» Wait for student response.

> *Awesome. I want to hear more about that later. Now, go on over to the centers area and find something fun. We'll start in a few minutes when everyone is here.*

Let the parents know when and where to return and explain that you will give them a debriefing at the end. Where possible save questions for the debrief.

Warm up Activity: 5 minutes

After all the students have arrived, gather them quickly into a fun active game. You want to keep instructions to a minimum, so choose a game that most children are familiar with. Tag is a good choice because it is well known, fun and you can get started quickly.

As you play, use your students' names as a reminder to the other students. "Good catch, Joe."

Social Skills Topic: 20 minutes

After no more than five minutes of the active game, direct everyone to the seating area. Welcome them back. Get started fast. Children with ASD will tune out quickly.

Hey everyone, welcome back to our social group. We will do our learning and role-play now for about 15 minutes. After that, we will play some more games.

2.1 Review last week's topic

Briefly review last week's learning. Cover the definition of 'shared interest', why we want to know shared interests, and the two types of questions we can use to find out shared interests.

*Let's review what we talked about last week. Do any of you remember what a **shared interest** is? We also called it a **common interest**.*

» Wait for student response.

Yes. A shared interest is a topic that both you and your friend are interested in. Something that both you and your friend like.

Now, which is more fun, talking about something you are both interested in, or talking about something that neither of you is interested in?

» Wait for student response.

Yeah. It is more fun talking about shared interests. Talking about things that you are not interested in is not as much fun.

We had a rule about talking that said something about shared interests. Does anyone remember that rule?

» Wait for student response.

> *Yes. Talk about shared interests. Because it's more FUN!*

» Write the rule on the whiteboard in section 1.

> *Okay, brainiacs. Let's see what else you remember. Last week, we learned two different question types to help us find out what our friends are interested in. Can anyone remember one of those questions?*

» Wait for student response. Give them enough time to think. If they give you a specific example, that is good enough. e.g. "What is your favorite movie?"

> *Yes. That's great. Let me write that question type up on the board.*

» Write the question on the board in the following format (depending on which was answered).

What is your favorite _____?

What did you do last_____? / What will you do next_____?

» Ask again to get the second question type and write it on the board once the students remember it.

> *Great job remembering what you did last week!*

2.2 Introduce the concept of a topic-starter question

Explain to students that a topic-starter question is a way to start talking with a friend about something he/she is interested in. Next, help students recall an interest for each student.

*After our work last week, we all know one or two of our friend's interests. This week we are going to learn how to start talking to our friends about their interests. We will learn how to do a **topic-starter** question.*

» Write Topic-starter question on the board.

First, let's remember our friend's interests. Who can remember something that Lisa is interested in?

» Wait for student response.

Continue asking questions until one interest for each student has been remembered.

Great remembering, everyone!

2.3 Topic-starter questions ask about our friend's interests

The first criteria for a topic-starter question is that it must be about something our friend is interested in.

Begin by drawing everyone's attention to a question you asked when you greeted one student.

Peter, can you remember the question I asked you when you arrived?

» Wait for student response.

Yes, I asked you if you went to Playland this week. I asked you that because I knew you were interested in Playland and planned to go this week.

That was a topic-starter question. It started a conversation with Peter.

» Choose a student who does not have the same interest.

> *Now, Kelly, should I ask you the same question about Playland that I asked Peter?*

» Wait for response.

> *Right. It doesn't make sense for me to ask you the same question because you are not interested in Playland like Peter is. I should ask you about what YOU are interested in.*
>
> *Let's write that down: Your question should be based on your friend's interests*

» Write on board: Ask about your friend's interests.

> *Let's see this in action to see what it looks like. Joe, go back to the door and come in again like you did at the beginning of class. I'm going to ask you a topic-starter question.*

» Wait for Joe to come in the door again. Greet him and ask him a topic-starter question. Let Joe respond appropriately.

> *Great! Thanks, Joe. You can sit down now.*
>
> *Okay, what was my topic-starter question?*

» Wait for student response.

> *Yes. I asked him about Minecraft. Did I ask him about something he is interested in?*

» Wait for student response.

Yes. Joe is interested in Minecraft so my topic-starter question met our rule.

Now, what if I also remembered that he planned on building a roller coaster in Minecraft this week. Can anyone think of an even better question I could have asked?

» Wait for student response.

Yes, I could have asked: Did you build that roller coaster you talked about last week?

That shows that I really listened to what he said last week. That will make him feel good. We want to make our friends feel good.

2.4 Topic-starter questions ask about recent activities

The second criteria for a topic-starter question is that it must be about recent or new information.

Right. Now, let me try a different topic-starter question on you. Peter, can you go across there and then pretend to join us again. The first time I asked you whether you went to Playland this week. This time, I am going to ask you a different topic-starter question.

» Wait for Peter to approach.

Hi, Peter. Did you go to Playland three years ago?

» Wait for student response.

» Point to the rule on the rule on the board about topic-starters being related to our friend's interests.

> *Okay, everyone. Was my question related to Peter's interests?*

» Wait for student response.

> *Yes, we know that Peter is interested in Playland, so the question is related to his interests.*
>
> *But, was there something a bit odd about my question?*

» Wait for student response. This will be a tough question, so feel free to give a high level of prompts or clues. Even with prompts, students may have no understanding that the question IS odd.

> *Yeah, I asked him about something that happened three years ago. It is a little odd to start a conversation about something that happened three years ago. We usually ask about things that have happened since we last saw our friend.*
>
> *Let's write that down as a rule.*

» Write on the board: Ask about what has happened since we last saw our friend.

> *So, what could I have asked instead?*

» Wait for students' response.

> *Yes. "Did you go to Playland this week?" is an excellent question.*
>
> *So, let's review. A good topic-starter question is...*

» Wait for student response.

Yes, a good topic-starter question is about our friend's interests. What else?

» Wait for student response.

Yes. A good topic-starter question asks about something recent... or about what has happened since we last saw our friend.

2.5 Teach when to do topic-starter questions

Part of generalizing a skill is teaching your learners when to apply the new skill. In this section you explain and demonstrate the various times when a topic-starter question is appropriate.

In a few minutes, we will practice some topic-starter questions.

But first, let's think about when we can use topic-starter questions. Any ideas for when to use topic-starter questions?

» Wait for student response(s). Note down good answers on the whiteboard. For incorrect answers, talk the student through to a good answer.

You want students to realize that topic-starter questions can be used anytime you are talking with a friend. Good conversations include relevant topic-starter questions.

When your students understand when they can use topic-starter questions, ask them what they can do if they don't remember any interests for a friend. The answer should be to ask one of the get-to-know-you questions that was introduced last week.

Keep in mind that this week's topic is focused on how to initiate a topic. We are not working on how to change a topic appropriately. That is a difficult skill and has its own lesson later in the course.

2.6 Role-play practice

The role-play practice ensures all students have a chance to demonstrate the new skill.

Great thinking, everyone. I think you are ready to practice some topic-starter questions yourself.

» Hand out the detective notes from Week 1.

Here are your detective notes from last week. You can use them to remind yourself about everyone's interests.

» Choose two students to stand up. Get one student to ask the other a topic-starter question.

Lisa & Joe, can you stand up, please?

Lisa, when I tell you, please walk over there and then come back and join the group. Peter, when Lisa comes back, I want you to greet her and ask a topic starter question.

Okay, Lisa, go and then come back to join the group.

Prompt as needed to facilitate the greeting, question and answer. Make sure the students do an appropriate greeting and greeting response before asking the topic-starter question. Also, make sure that the question is related to Lisa's interests and recent activity.

Excellent, thanks, Lisa and Peter. You can sit down now.

Now, what was Peter's topic-starter question?

» Wait for student response.

Yes, he asked her about playing Pokémon Go.

Let's check our rules. Was the question about something that Lisa is interested in?

» Wait for student response.

> *Yes. We know that Lisa is interested in Pokémon Go.*
>
> *Next, (point to the board), did Peter asked about something recent to do with Pokémon Go?*

» Wait for student response.

> *Yes. He asked what level she is at now. Nice job, Peter!*

Choose another two students to repeat the same role-play. Continue until all students have taken both roles. Where possible, get students to ask original questions and not repeat questions that have previously been asked.

Practice Activity: 10 minutes

The practice activity gives students more highly-supported practice at demonstrating the new skill. This is an important step towards getting them to demonstrate the skill during the more natural game-based activities in the remainder of the session.

> *Fantastic work, everyone! Next, I'd like you to all stand up. You have each asked a topic-starter question to one person. Take your detective notes and put a checkmark next to that person's name.*

» Wait for students to put the checkmark next to the correct name.

> *Now, look at your notes and ask a topic-starter question to a different student. Let them answer the question and then just keep talking on that topic if you can.*
>
> *When you are done, put a check against their name. Continue until you have a checkmark against everyone's name.*

Watch and support as needed as students complete the activity.

> *Awesome job, everyone! Guess what is next...? Yes, snack!*
>
> *During snack, I would like you to talk to each other. And remember: Topic-starter questions can be used while you are having snack, playing games, any time you are with someone.*
>
> *So, if no one is talking, ask someone a topic-starter question.*
>
> *Let's go!*

Snack Break: 15 minutes

Get snack started. Then briefly mark the assessment sheet for the previous activity. You will note whether each student needed no support, some support or a lot of support to complete the activity.

During the snack break, if the students talk to each other, stay in the background. If there is no talking, or if one or two students are not talking, prompt the conversation similar to the following.

> *Hey, everyone, it's pretty quiet here. Peter, can you think of a question you can ask Joe?*

If necessary, remind Peter about Joe's interests.

Also, watch out for students asking the same question that they asked this student before. You can prompt as follows.

> *Hey Lisa, didn't you ask Peter that question before? So, you already know the answer to that question.*
>
> *We don't ask questions if we already know the answer. Can you think of a different question you can ask Peter?*

If necessary, remind Lisa about Peter's interests.

Board Game Activity: 20 minutes

Have a selection of 3 board games available. These should be fast-moving games that take only 10-15 minutes to play. Students should have fun while they play.

Ask your students to decide amongst themselves which game to play. The decision should take less than a minute. Prompt as needed to help the children develop the skill of making a group decision.

Only the students play the game. During the game, your job is to monitor and prompt good game behavior - taking turns, being fair, being supportive, etc.

If possible, also encourage conversation in the same way as you did during snack, by prompting for a topic-starter question.

If you have a chance, complete the assessment for the snack activity.

Towards the end, fill in the assessment sheet for this activity. You will note the level of support the student needed to play the game: no support, some support or lots of support. You will also note if each student successfully initiated conversation based on your explicit prompt or if they initiated conversation without prompting.

If the game is going well, continue it without comment. If the game is not successful, finish it early.

> *Hey, we have run out of time for this today. Let's pack up and get on to our next activity. I think you'll love it!*

Game Show: 20 minutes

As we move into the last third of the session, we again introduce the high-energy game show. The activity gives students practice at asking a variety of topic-starter questions. The speed of the game show encourages fluency at this skill.

Don't be shy of being an "over the top" game show host if it gets your students engaged.

> *For our next activity, we are going to play a game show like last week. Here are your buzzers.*

» Hand out the buzzers.

> *Everyone, try out your buzzer. Yep. All good.*
>
> *All right. Get ready to listen to the first question. If you know the answer, press your buzzer. If you yell out the answer, your answer doesn't count. So what do you need to do if you know the answer?*

» Wait for student response.

> *Yes. You press the buzzer. Okay, here is the first question. I have a friend named Michael. He does gymnastics three times a week. I haven't seen him for a month. What is a good topic-starter question?*

» Wait for student response. Ask the first person to buzz for their answer.

Continue asking questions like the following. (See complete question list in Appendix B.)

> *I have a friend/aunt/uncle who likes _____. I haven't seen him/her for a few days/weeks/months. What is a good topic starter question?*
>
> *I haven't seen my friend _____ over the summer. We see each other on the first day of school. What is a good conversation starter?*
>
> *My mom goes to book club once per month. What can I ask her when she gets home?*
>
> *My dad plays hockey every Friday night. What can I ask him when I see him on Saturday morning?*
>
> *I run into my friend ___ at the library/coffee shop/park/playground. I haven't seen him for a year, and I can't remember what he is interested in. What can I ask him after I have said "Hi" to him?*

If possible, seek out more detailed topic-starter questions. For example:

> *Coach: I have a friend Gina who loves ballet. She had a ballet competition last week. What is a good topic-starter question?*
>
> *Student: Hey Gina. How is your ballet class going?*
>
> *Coach: Excellent. That is a great question. Now, how can we make it even better? Remember, she had a competition last week.*
>
> *Student: Hey Gina. How was your ballet competition last week?*
>
> *Coach: Yes. That question is even better because it shows we remember more details about our friend. We remember not just that she likes ballet, but that she also had a competition last week. That shows your friend that you are really interested in her. That will make her feel good.*

As time for this activity runs out, finish up the game show.

> *Fantastic job, everyone! You are doing some great topic-starter questions.*
>
> *Now, tell me again, when can we use topic-starter questions?*

» Wait for student response.

> *Yes. We can use them whenever we are talking to someone. And what are our two rules for topic-starter questions?*

» Wait for student response.

> *Yes. The question must be about our friend's interests.*

» Seek additional information and wait for student response.

> *Yes. The question should be about recent activities.*

Group Activity: 15 minutes

Identify whether you want your students to do a board game, active game, craft or building activity. Your choice will depend on the energy level and current behavior of your students.

Once you have identified the type of game, give your students a choice of 3 options and get them to decide between them what they want to do.

Only the students engage in the activity. Your job is to monitor and prompt good game behavior - taking turns, being fair, being supportive, etc.

If possible, also encourage conversation in the same way as previously, by prompting for a topic-starter question.

If you have a chance, complete the game show assessment.

Towards the end, fill in the assessment sheet for this activity

As parents start to arrive, finish up the activity, unless it is one the students can continue without support.

> *Okay, let's pack up this game. Once we are done, I'd like you to go over to the centers area. You will find craft materials and building blocks. Choose anything you'd like to do while I tell your parents how awesomely you did today.*

Parent Debrief: 10 minutes

The purpose of the parent debrief is to educate them about the specific skills taught this lesson, introduce the homework assignment and answer any questions they may have.

All of the required information is in the parent handout for this week. Please use that as your prompt for the debrief.

Post Session

Take 5 minutes to review your assessment, adding in any extra data or notes that you couldn't do during the session. Consider the following questions for each student.

Did this student successfully ask a topic-starter question that was relevant to their conversation partner?

Did this student demonstrate independent use of this skill during the structured activities of the group session?

Week 3
Making Comments

Background

This week your students learn how to make an appropriate comment when their friend says something or does something. A comment is when you say something nice to show you listened.

Your students will learn the following rules about comments:

- Comment when your friend does something or says something.
- Match the comment to the information.

e.g. Happy comments for happy information. Sad comments for sad information.

Lesson Content

Preparation:

» Set up your space to suit your needs. Ideally, you will have a sitting area, a centers area, and an active area.
» In your centers area, set up craft, building and board game stations.
» Bring something of your own that shows a skill. For example, juggling bags, a kendama, a cool trick, a coin to flip and catch in a cup... anything! You will quickly demonstrate this so that students can make a comment.

» If you have access to a smartphone or iPad, load a quick-moving game like Geometry Dash.

» Print the sign that says **Ask me a topic-starter question**. Print the Topic diagram. See Appendix D for all signs and diagrams.

» Photocopy the Week 3 Conversation Sentences from Appendix B. Cut the sentences into strips and put the sentences into a container so they can be picked randomly.

» You will need a copy of the Week 3 assessment sheet as well as a parent handout for each child.

» Make sure you have a snack ready to serve, but keep it out of view until snack time.

Settle in: 5 Minutes

Probe: Topic-starter question

As students arrive, greet them and show them your sign that says **Ask me a topic-starter question**. You may need to ask other students to wait their turn to come in.

Here are examples for successful and unsuccessful students.

Successful

> *Coach: Hey, Joe. (Show the sign.)*

» Wait for student response.

> *Student: Hi Jake. Ummmm... Did you play Mario Kart this week?*
>
> *Coach: Yeah, I did! Great question, Joe. Can you head over to the centers area? We'll get started soon.*

Unsuccessful

> *Coach: Hey, Joe. (Show the sign.)*

Wait for student response.

Student: Hi Jake. Ummmm... Ummm...

Coach: Do you remember anything I am interested in?

Student: Not really.

Coach: No problem! What question can you ask me if you don't remember any of my interests?

Student: Ummmm...

Coach: You can ask me a get-to-know-you question. Maybe ask about my weekend?

Student: What did you do on the weekend?

Coach: Great question! I went kayaking. It was awesome. Let's talk more about that later. Can you head over to the centers area? We'll get started soon. I can see Lisa is there already. Think about what topic-starter question you can ask her after you say "Hi."

Let the parents know what time to return and explain that you will give them a debriefing then. Where possible save questions for the debrief.

Warm up Activity: 5 minutes

After all the students have arrived, gather them quickly into a fun active game. Since students are more comfortable now, you could introduce a new game. Remember to keep it simple because you want this activity to last no more than 5 minutes.

Social Skills Topic: 20 minutes

After no more than five minutes of the active game, direct everyone to the seating area. Welcome them back. As usual, get started fast. Children with ASD will tune out quickly.

> *Hey everyone, welcome back to our social skills group. We will do our learning and role-play now for about 15 minutes. After that, we will play some more games.*

3.1 Briefly review topic-starter questions

Briefly cover topic-starter questions from last week, noting especially the criteria of "interesting to our friend" and "about something recent."

> *You all did a great job asking me a topic-starter question when you came in. Now, did anyone use a topic-starter question at the centers?*

If yes:

> *Joe, you asked Lisa a question? Fantastic! What question did you ask?*

» Wait for Joe's response.

> *Great. And why was that a good question for Lisa?*

» Elicit the fact that Joe's question met the criteria for topic-starter questions: The topic is interesting to our friend and is about something recent.

» If other students asked questions, follow up similarly.

If no:

> *No questions? Oh, no! Let's practice some now. Pete, what question could you ask Joe?*

Prompt two or three students through the process of asking appropriate topic-starter questions. Refer to Week 2 for details about topic-starter questions.

3.2 Demonstrate comments & introduce relevance rule

Demonstrate comments and introduce the idea that the comment must match what your friend said. Positive comments for positive information. Negative comments for negative information.

> *All right! Let's move on. This week we are going to learn about making comments.*
>
> *Comments are what we say when someone tells us something.*
>
> *Joe, tell me something you did on the weekend.*

» Wait for student response, then make an appropriate comment. For example:

> *Hey, that sounds great. Where did you go kayaking?*

» Write your comment on the board. Make sure it includes the comment and the follow-up question.

» Circle the comment.

> *This is the comment I made when Joe told me he went kayaking. I said, "Hey, that sounds great."*
>
> *Did that seem like a good thing to say?*

» Wait for student response.

> *Yeah. It was a good thing to say. Let's redo that conversation with a different comment.*

> *Hey Joe, what did you do on the weekend?*

» Wait for student response.

> *Oh, that's too bad. (Exaggerate sadness.)*
>
> *Okay, what was wrong with that comment?*

» Wait for student response.

> *Yes. The comment did not match what Joe told me. When you make a comment, it needs to match what your friend told you.*
>
> *Let's write that on the board to help us remember.*

» Write on board: Match comment to information.

> *Let's brainstorm some more comments that we could make when Joe tells us he went kayaking.*

» Prompt and encourage until you have 3-5 appropriate comments. Write them on the board.

> *That's great! Now, what if I told you this: My dog died on the weekend.*
>
> *What sort of comments are okay in this situation?*

» Prompt and encourage until you have 3-5 appropriate comments. Write them on the board.

Good job. Your comments would make me feel better if my dog had died. Luckily, my dog is fine!

» Point at the comments.

As you can see, your comment must relate to what your friend has told you.

3.3 Introduce rule: Comment when your friend says something or does something

Children with ASD often don't realize that they need to comment or acknowledge when their friend has said something. In this section you give them a simple rule to follow. Where possible, use a gestural prompt instead of a verbal prompt to indicate when a student needs to add a comment.

So far we've been making comments when someone says something. We also make comments when someone does something. Watch me.

Do your trick, kendama catch, juggling or whatever particular talent you choose to demonstrate. When you have done something cool, look at the students expectantly. You want them to make a comment. If necessary, prompt.

Did anyone think that was cool?

» Wait for student response.

Yeah? Then tell me! Make a comment.

» Wait for student response.

Thanks! That was a nice comment.

So, when do we comment? When our friend says something or when he...

» Wait for student response.

Yes. We comment when our friend says something or does something. Let's write that on the board.

» Write the rule on the board: Comment when your friend says something or does something.

So, why do you think it is a good idea to comment when someone says something or does something?

» Wait for student response. Students may not know why commenting is needed.

Yes. It's a good idea to comment because it shows our friend that we are listening. It shows we are interested. We need to do that or our friend will think we are not interested and will go and talk to someone else!

So, we need to remember to comment when our friend says something or does something. When we comment, our friend will know we are listening.

3.4 Role-play practice

The role-play practice ensures all students have a chance to demonstrate the new skill.

» Grab the bowl of conversation sentences that you prepared during prep time.

Let's practice making comments. Lisa, pick a sentence from this bowl and tell it to Joe. Joe, you will need to make an appropriate comment.

Wait for students to perform the task. If needed, prompt to help each student produce an appropriate comment.

Great comment! Now Joe, your turn. Pick a sentence and tell Kelly. Kelly, it will be your turn to comment.

» Wait for student response. Prompt, if needed.

Choose another two students to repeat the same role-play. Continue until all students have taken both roles. Where possible, get students to produce original comments and not repeat comments that have previously been used.

Fantastic work, everyone! Now, let's see how comments fit in with what we have learned in previous lessons.

Display the following diagram from Appendix D or draw it on the whiteboard.

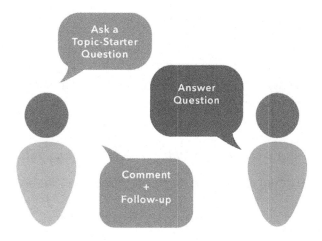

Take a look at this picture. Here's how it works.

» Point to the first speech bubble:

You can start or continue a conversation by asking a topic-starter question.

» Point to the second speech bubble.

Your friend then answers the question.

» Point to the last speech bubble.

You then make a comment.

After the comment, you can ask a follow-up question about what your friend told you. We'll become experts at follow-up questions next week. For this week, we are just going to practice the first three steps up until the comment, though you can ask a follow-up question if you want to!

Practice Activity: 10 minutes

This activity gives students more highly-supported practice at demonstrating the new skill. This is an important step towards getting them to use the skill during the more natural game-based activities in the remainder of the session.

I'd like you to all stand up. I am going to put you into pairs and call you Person 1 or Person 2. You are going to practice doing the three steps in the diagram.

Person 1 will ask a topic-starter question. Person 2 will answer the question. Person 1 will make a comment.

> *Lisa and Joe, come over here. Lisa, you are Person 1. Joe, you are Person 2. Who is going to ask the topic-starter question?*

» Wait for student response.

> *Yes, Lisa will ask the topic-starter question. Who will answer the question?*

» Wait for student response.

> *Yes. Joe will answer the question. Who will make a comment?*

» Wait for student response.

> *Yes. Lisa will make a comment. All right. Luke and Kelly, you can go over there. Luke, you are Person 1. Kelly, you are Person 2.*
>
> *Start when you are ready.*

Support students through the process. Have your **Comment** sign to show as a visual prompt if a student forgets to comment.

Get students to swap roles when they are done. If there is time, change pairs and redo.

> *Awesome job, everyone! Guess what is next...? Yes, snack! During snack, I would like you to practice this 3-step process with each other.*
>
> *So, if no one is talking, ask someone a topic-starter question. And when someone says something, make a comment.*
>
> *Let's go!*

Snack Break: 15 minutes

Get snack started. Then briefly mark the assessment sheet for the previous activity. Note whether each student needed no support, some support or a lot of support to complete the activity.

During the snack break, if the students talk to each other, stay in the background. If there is no talking, or if one or two students are not talking, prompt the conversation with the following:

> *Hey everyone, it's pretty quiet here. Peter, can you think of a question you can ask*
>
> *Joe?*

If necessary, remind Peter about Joe's interests. Keep your **Comment** sign handy to prompt as needed.

Also, watch out for students asking the same question that they asked this student before.

Board Game Activity: 20 minutes

Grab three board games from your collection. Ask your students to decide amongst themselves which game to play. Get the game started, explaining as needed to those unfamiliar with the game.

Only the students play the game. During the game, your job is to monitor and prompt good game behavior - taking turns, being fair, being supportive, etc.

Encourage conversation during the game, making sure that appropriate comments are made.

A board game is an excellent time to practice commenting after a player does something. e.g. "Lucky roll", "Good guess", etc.

If you have a chance, complete the assessment for the snack activity.

Towards the end, fill in the assessment sheet for this activity. You will note the level of support the student needed to play the game: no support, some support or lots of support. You will also note how much prompting each student needed to successfully comment.

If the game is going well, let it continue. If the game is not successful, finish it early.

Game Show: 20 minutes

Again, we energize the last half of the session with a game show. This week's questions help students rapidly come up with appropriate comments.

> *For our last activity, we are going to play a game show like last week. Here are your buzzers.*

» Hand out the buzzers.

> *Everyone, try out your buzzer. Yep. All good.*
>
> *I will give you a statement, and you need to make an appropriate comment.*
>
> *All right. Get ready to listen to the first statement. If you can think of a comment, press your buzzer. If you yell out the answer, your answer doesn't count. So what do you need to do if you know the answer?*

» Wait for student response.

> *Yes. You press the buzzer.*

» Select a statement from your bowl of conversation sentences.

> *Okay, here is the first statement: Guess what, I got a new bike on the weekend!*

» Wait for student response. Ask the first person to buzz for their comment

Continue choosing statements from your container. Feel free to make up additional ones to suit your students' interests.

If your students are doing really well with comments, get them to ask a follow-up question as well. We will learn about follow-up questions next week, so don't worry if you feel it is best to stick with practicing comments this week.

When it is time, finish up the game show.

Final Group Activity: 15 Minutes

If you have a smartphone or iPad, your students will be ecstatic about this week's final activity. Choose a "platformer" type game where the player tries to pass a level. Geometry Dash is a great choice because turns are over pretty quickly.

Make sure all students understand how to play the game and then get them taking one turn at a time, passing it quickly when they die.

This situation is perfect for practicing comments. Encourage students to comment positively on the current player's performance and to commiserate when things go badly. Encourage them to make at least one comment per turn, for faster moving games. Set your goal higher if a turn lasts longer.

If you do not have access to a smartphone or iPad, follow the instructions from Week 2 for the final activity.

Parent Debrief: 10 minutes

The purpose of the parent debrief is to educate the parents about the specific skills taught this lesson, introduce the homework assignment and answer any questions they may have.

All of the required information is in the parent handout for this week. Please use that as your prompt for the debrief.

Post Session

Take 5 minutes to review your assessment, adding in any extra data or notes that you couldn't complete during the session. Consider the following question for each student.

> Did this student successfully make comments that were appropriate?

Week 4
Follow-up Questions

Background

This week your students learn learned how to ask an appropriate follow-up question when their friend has said something. A follow-up question is a question that is related to the current topic of conversation. Students will practice follow-up questions in isolation and then as part of a natural conversation.

Some examples of appropriate follow-up questions are:

> A: I went to Playland yesterday!

> B: That sounds like fun! What rides did you go on?

> A: We went camping on the weekend.

> B: Cool. Where did you go?

Follow-up questions are often preceded by a brief comment, as illustrated in the previous examples.

Lesson Content

Preparation:

> » Set up your space to suit your needs. Ideally, you will have a sitting area, a centers area and an active area.

» In your centers area, set up craft, building and board game stations.

» Have your **Comment** sign, the **Comment + Follow-up** sign and topic diagram ready. You will use the signs as a visual prompt if needed. The diagram will be used as part of the lesson. All signs and diagrams can be found in Appendix D.

» You will need a copy of the Week 4 assessment sheet as well as a parent handout for each child.

» Make sure you have a snack ready to serve, but keep it out of view until snack time.

Settle in: 5 Minutes

Probe: Comments

As students arrive, greet them and say something interesting, like "Hey Joe, guess what, I went to the movies yesterday!"

Wait for the student to comment. If they don't, prompt them with your **Comment** sign.

After the student has successfully commented, direct the student to the centers area.

Let the parents know what time to return and explain that you will give them a debriefing then. Where possible save questions for the debrief.

Warm up Activity: 5 minutes

After all the students have arrived, gather them quickly into a fun active game. Since your students are more comfortable now, you could introduce a new game. Remember to keep it simple because you want this activity to last no more than 5 minutes.

Social Skills Topic: 20 minutes

After no more than five minutes of the active game, direct everyone to the seating area. Welcome them back. As usual, get started fast. Children with ASD will tune out quickly.

Hey everyone, welcome back to our social group. We will do our learning and role-play now for about 15 minutes. After that, we will play some more games.

4.1 Briefly review conversation table from last time

Review the conversation diagram from last week.

» Display topic diagram from Appendix D.

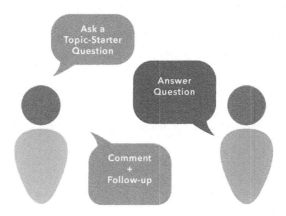

Does everyone remember this picture from last time? It shows us how conversations work.

» Point as you explain:

The first person asks a topic-starter question. The second person answers the question. The first person then makes a comment and asks a follow-up question.

In Week 2 we learned about topic-starter questions. Last week we learned about making comments. Can anyone guess what we are going to practice this week?

» Wait for student response.

Yes. We are going to practice follow-up questions.

4.2 Introduce Follow-up Questions

Introduce the idea of a follow-up question where you ask for more information on the same topic. Make sure students understand and can demonstrate that there are a variety of follow-up questions that can be asked in any given situation. There is not one "right" follow-up question.

> *A follow-up question is when you ask for more information **on the same topic**. Let me write that on the board.*

» Write: Follow-up Question = Ask for more information on the same topic.

> *Let me show you an example.*

Choose a student who had a successful interaction when you greeted them. If possible, ask a different topic-starter question. You do not want your students to think it is okay to have the same conversation more than once.

> *Okay, Kelly. Can you stand up? I am going to ask you a topic-starter question.*

» Wait for Kelly to stand.

> *Kelly, what did you do on the weekend?*

» Wait for student response.

> *Wow, that sounds really interesting. What movie did you see?*

» Wait for student to answer.

> *Thanks, Kelly. You can sit down now.*

So, what was my topic-starter question? (Point to topic diagram.)

» Wait for student response.

Yes. I asked her about her weekend. She answered that she went to the movies.

What was my comment? (Point to topic diagram.)

» Wait for student response.

Yes. I said that sounded really interesting.

What was my follow-up question? (Point to topic diagram.)

» Wait for student response.

If students cannot correctly recall the parts of the conversation, write the conversation on the board. Now that students can see the conversation, ask which is the topic-starter, etc.

Yes, I asked what movie she saw.

Awesome. Was my question about the same topic that she was talking about?

» Wait for student response.

Yes. She mentioned she went to the movies, so I asked her what movie she saw.

Let's practice some more follow-up questions. Joe, what follow-up question could you ask if I said I went skiing on the weekend?

» Wait for student response.

Great! Can anyone think of another follow-up question to ask me?

Help students brainstorm a variety of follow-up questions to that one statement from you. It is important for them to know that there is a variety of things they can question: where you went, who you went with, how you enjoyed it, etc. Any of those are great follow-up questions.

Guide the students to make sure that their follow-up questions stay appropriately on the same topic. Some possible problems are:

- The student asks an off-topic question: Why didn't you go swimming?
- The student focuses only on how the topic relates to their special interest: Did you drink pop while you were there?

Use the following scenarios and get the students to brainstorm a variety of appropriate follow-up questions.

- I went bowling on the weekend.
- I saw my grandparents on the weekend.
- I went to the zoo on the weekend.

Great job everyone! I think you are ready to do this yourself! Let's try.

4.3 Role-play Practice

The role-play practice ensures all students have a chance to demonstrate the new skill.

One at a time, get students to practice the 3-step conversations. Let the second student answer the follow-up question and then switch the students.

Continue until each student has had a turn asking the topic-starter question and being the one who answers the topic-starter question.

Prompt and guide as needed for success for each student.

Practice Activity: 10 minutes

This activity gives students more highly-supported practice at demonstrating the new skill. This is an important step towards getting them to independently use the skill during the more natural game-based activities in the remainder of the session.

> *Fantastic work, everyone! Next I'd like you to all stand up. I am going to put you into pairs and call you Person 1 or Person 2. You are going to practice doing these three steps.*
>
> *Person 1 will ask a topic-starter question. Person 2 will answer the question. Person 1 will make a comment and ask a follow-up question.*
>
> *Lisa and Joe, come over here. Lisa, you are Person 1. Joe you are Person 2. Who is going to ask the topic-starter question?*

» Wait for student response.

> *Yes, Lisa will ask the topic-starter question. Who will answer the question?*

» Wait for student response.

> *Yes. Joe will answer the question. Who will make a comment and ask a follow-up question?*

» Wait for student response.

> *Yes. Lisa will make a comment. All right. Peter and Kelly, you can go over there. Peter you are Person 1. Kelly you are Person 2.*
>
> *Start when you are ready.*

Support students through the process. Get them to swap roles when they are done. If there is time, change pairs and redo. Use your visual prompt signs when necessary.

> *Awesome job, everyone! Guess what is next? Yes, snack! During snack I would like you to practice this 3-step process with each other.*
>
> *So, if no one is talking, ask someone a topic-starter question.*
>
> *Let's go!*

Snack Break: 15 minutes

Get snack started. Then briefly mark the assessment sheet for the previous activity. You will note whether each student needed no support, some support or a lot of support to complete the activity.

During the snack break, if the students talk to each other, stay in the background. If there is no talking, or if one or two students are not talking, prompt the conversation similar to the following.

> *Hey everyone, it's pretty quiet here. Peter, ask Kelly what she did on the weekend.*

Prompt the students to comment and follow-up on Kelly's answer.

Also watch out for students asking the same question that they asked this student before.

Board Game Activity: 20 minutes

Grab a selection of three games from your collection. This week is a good time to introduce a new game if you have one available. Let the students decide which game to play.

Get the game started. Encourage conversation in the usual way. Prompt where appropriate to encourage comments and follow-up questions. Also ensure that general commenting happens, such as "Good choice," "Well done," etc.

Towards the end, fill in the assessment sheet for this activity.

If the game is going well, continue it without comment. If the game is not successful, finish it early.

Game Show: 20 minutes

During this week's game show, the students must come up with appropriate comments and follow-up questions.

> *For our next activity, we are going to play a game show like last week. Here are your buzzers.*

» Hand out the buzzers.

> *Everyone, try out your buzzer. Yep. All good.*
>
> *I will give you a statement and you need to make an appropriate comment and ask a follow-up question.*
>
> *All right. Get ready to listen to the first statement. If you can think of a comment and follow-up question, press your buzzer. If you yell out the answer, your answer doesn't count.*
>
> *Select a statement from your bowl of conversation sentences.*
>
> *Okay, here is the first statement: Guess what, I got a new bike on the weekend!*

» Wait for student response. Ask the first person to buzz for their comment and follow-up question.

Continue choosing statements from your container. Feel free to make up additional ones to suit your students' interests.

> *Fantastic job, everyone! You are asking some great follow-up questions.*

Final Group Activity: 15 Minutes

Depending on the energy of your group, decide whether they will do a board game, craft activity, building activity or an active game. Once you have decided on the type of game, give them a choice of three and get them to decide amongst themselves.

Your role is to observe, prompt when needed to ensure comments, and complete the assessment sheet.

Parent Debrief: 10 minutes

The purpose of the parent debrief is to educate them about the specific skills taught this lesson, introduce the homework assignment and answer any questions they may have.

All of the required information is in the parent handout for this week. Please use that as your prompt for the debrief.

Post Session

Take 5 minutes to review your assessment, adding in any extra data or notes that you couldn't complete during the session. Consider the following question for each student:

> Did this student successfully ask follow-up questions that were appropriate?

Week 5
Follow-up Comments

Background

This week students practice follow-up comments. In a follow-up comment, the speaker extends his comment by adding some personal information relevant to what was just said. Students will practice extended comments in isolation and then as part of a natural conversation.

Follow-up comments are typically used as an alternative to follow-up questions.

Lesson Content

Preparation:

» Set up your space to suit your needs. Ideally you will have a sitting area, a centers area and an active area.
» In your centers area, set up craft, building and board game stations.
» Print out the **Comment + Follow-up** sign from Appendix D. This will be used as a visual prompt.
» Print out the Conversation Questions from the Week 5 materials in Appendix B. Cut them up and put them in a bowl. Make another bowl of the Conversation Statements from last week.
» You will need a copy of the Week 5 assessment sheet as well as a parent handout for each child.

» Make sure you have a snack ready to serve, but keep it out of view until snack time.

Settle in: 5 Minutes

Probe: Follow-up questions

As students arrive, greet them and tell them something interesting. Wait for them to respond with a comment and a follow-up question. If needed, show them your sign.

For example:

> Coach: Hey Lisa, guess what, I went camping on the weekend.
>
> Lisa: Awesome.... <sees your prompt>... Ummm... That's cool. Where did you go?
>
> Coach: I went to Galliano Island. It was great. How about you head over to the centers area. We'll get started in a few minutes.

If a student inadvertently does a follow-up comment instead of a follow-up question, that is perfectly okay. Praise and continue.

Let the parents know what time to return and explain that you will give them a debriefing then. Where possible save questions for the debrief.

Warm up Activity: 5 minutes

After all the students have arrived, gather them quickly into a fun active game. Since students are more comfortable now, you could introduce a new game. Remember to keep it simple because you want this activity to last no more than 5 minutes.

Social Skills Topic: 20 minutes

After no more than five minutes of warm up, direct everyone to the seating area. Welcome them back. As usual, get started fast.

> Hey everyone, welcome back to our social group. We will do our learning and role-play now for about 15 minutes. After that, we will play some more games.

5.1 Briefly review conversation diagram from last time

Review the conversation diagram from last time, covering all the steps that have been taught so far: topic-starter questions, comments and follow-up questions.

» Display topic diagram.

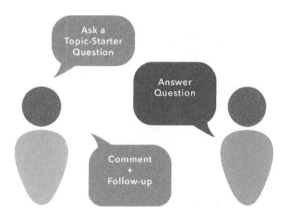

Does everyone remember this picture from last time? It shows us how conversations work.

» Point as you explain:

The first person asks a topic-starter question. The second person answers the question. The first person then makes a comment and asks a follow-up question.

This is one way that conversations can work.

We learned and practiced follow-up questions last week. And today you all did a great job asking a follow-up question when we greeted each other at the door. Well done!

This week we are going to learn something new. A follow-up comment.

5.2 Introduce Follow-up Comments

Explain to students that follow-up comments allow the speaker to share information from their own knowledge and experience. Follow-up comments should convey new information and be related to the current topic of conversation.

> *A follow-up comment is when you add some **new** information to the conversation. And it has to be **related** to what was just said. Let's write that on the board.*

» Write **New** and **Related** on the whiteboard.

> *Now, let's practice: Joe, what did you have for dinner last night?*

» Wait for Joe to respond to the question.

> *Yum. That sounds great. I had fish and chips for dinner.*

» Write your response on the whiteboard. First circle the initial comment.

> *Here's my first comment. Yum. That sounds great.*

» Now circle the follow-up comment.

> *This is my follow-up comment. I had fish and chips for dinner.*

» Point to the word **New** on the whiteboard.

> *Does my comment tell you new information?*

» Wait for student response.

Yes. It gives you new information you didn't know before - what I had for dinner last night.

» Point to the word **Related** on the whiteboard.

Now, is my comment related to the conversation? **Related** *means it is about the same topic.*

» Wait for student response.

Yes. I asked Joe about what he had for dinner. So what I had for dinner is related.

Now, watch this conversation. Lisa, what did you have for dinner?

» Wait for Lisa's response.

Yum. That sounds delicious. I'm going to the movies tomorrow.

Did I give you new information?

» Wait for student response.

Yes. That information about going to the movies was new. Now, was my follow-up comment related to the conversation?

» Wait for student response.

No. It wasn't. We were talking about what we had for dinner last night and I added information about what I plan to do tomorrow.

> *So that wasn't a good follow-up comment.*
>
> *Let's try again. I had pizza for dinner last night. Kelly, what did you have for dinner last night?*

» Wait for Kelly's response.

> *Oh, I love spaghetti. I had pizza for dinner last night.*
>
> *Okay, everyone. What was wrong with my follow-up comment?*

» Wait for student response.

> *You are correct. My follow-up comment did not provide new information. I had already told you that I had pizza for dinner. I shouldn't tell you again!*

» Point at the board.

> *Your follow-up comment must be new and related.*
>
> *Let's practice a few. Lisa, you will be first. I will say something and then you need to do a follow-up comment.*

» Choose a conversation sentence from the bowl and read it aloud.

» Wait for Lisa's response.

Comment/correct as needed. Give each student a chance to practice a follow-up comment.

Keep in mind that follow-up comments can be quite simple. For example:

> *A: I don't like this music.*

> *B: Me either.*

In this example, the brief two-word follow-up comment conveys information that is new and related.

5.3 When to use follow-up comment versus follow-up question

Let students know that they can do a follow-up question OR a follow-up comment.

> *Wow, you are all doing a great job with follow-up comments.*
>
> *Now, last week you learned how to do a follow-up **question**. This week you learned how to do a follow-up **comment**.*
>
> *How do you decide which one to use?*

» Wait for student response. They may not know the answer.

> *There are no rules for which one to use! Use whatever suits the conversation. The best thing to keep in mind is to mix it up so sometimes you are asking a question and sometimes you are making a comment.*
>
> *What could happen if you asked follow-up questions ALL the time?*

» Wait for student response.

> *Yeah. It might seem like you are asking too many questions.*
>
> *What could happen if your NEVER asked a follow-up question?*

» Wait for student response.

Yes. It might seem like you are not interested in your friend because you aren't asking for more information.

Your best bet is to mix it up.

5.4 Role-play practice

The role-play practice ensures all students have a chance to demonstrate the new skill.

Get your bowl of conversation questions for the students to choose from.

Let's practice some follow-up comments, then we'll mix it up a bit. Peter, grab a question from the bowl and ask Joe. When he replies, make a comment and then a follow-up comment.

Prompt the students as needed to support. Switch students until everyone has had a turn to practice making follow-up comments.

Next, repeat the exercise but allow the students to make a follow-up question or a follow-up comment.

Practice Activity: 10 minutes

This activity gives students more highly-supported practice at demonstrating the new skill. This is an important step towards getting them to independently use the skill during the more natural game-based activities in the remainder of the session.

Fantastic work everyone! Next, I'd like you to all stand up. I am going to put you into pairs and call you Person 1 or Person 2. You are going to practice doing follow-up comments and questions. If you are Person 1, you can choose your own question or grab one from the bowl here.

> *I'd like you to continue the conversation for a few turns, so keep talking back and forth.*
>
> *Start when you are ready.*

Support students through the process. Get them to swap roles when they are done. If there is time, change pairs and redo.

> *Awesome job! Guess what is next...? Yes, snack!*
>
> *During snack I would like you to talk to each other. You can use follow-up questions or follow-up comments. Whatever seems right.*
>
> *Let's go!*

Snack Break: 15 minutes

Get snack started. Then briefly mark the assessment sheet for the previous activity. You will note whether each student needed no support, some support or a lot of support to complete the activity.

During the snack break, if the students talk to each other, stay in the background. If there is no talking, or if one or two students are not talking, prompt the conversation.

Board Game Activity: 20 minutes

Have a selection of three board games available. These should be fast-moving games that take only 10-15 minutes to play. Students should have fun while they play. Ask your students to decide amongst themselves which game to play.

Get the game started, explaining as needed to those unfamiliar with the game. During the game, your job is to monitor and prompt good game behavior - taking turns, being fair, being supportive, etc.

If possible, also encourage conversation in the same way as you did during snack. Provide praise for:

   - Topic-starter questions

- Comments
- Follow-up questions
- Follow-up comments
- Continuing beyond the first few turns in a conversation

Towards the end, fill in the assessment sheet for this activity. You will note the level of support the student needed to play the game: no support, some support or lots of support. You will also note in general how students are doing at conversing while playing a game.

If the game is going well, continue it without comment. If the game is not successful, finish it early.

Game Show: 20 minutes

The gameshow this week will focus on making follow-up comments. The fast pace helps students think quickly and develops their fluency at coming up with follow-up comments. Use the bowl of conversation sentences.

Our next activity is the game show! Here are your buzzers.

» Hand out the buzzers and set expectations as in previous weeks.

Everyone ready?

I will give you a sentence and you need to make an appropriate comment and follow-up comment.

Okay, here is the first statement: Guess what, I got a new bike on the weekend!

Wait for student response. Ask the first person to buzz for their comment. If appropriate, give them a point.

Continue choosing statements from your container of topic sentences. Feel free to make up additional ones to suit your students' interests.

When time is up:

Fantastic job, everyone! You are make some great follow-up comments.

Final Group Activity: 15 Minutes

Depending on the energy of your group, decide whether they will do a board game, craft activity, building activity or an active game. You might also consider doing a video game like the platformer game introduced in Week 3. Taking turns and watching video games is an excellent environment for practicing follow-up comments.

Parent Debrief: 10 minutes

Conduct the parent debrief as usual The required information is contained in the parent handout for this week.

Post Session

Take five minutes to review your assessment, adding in any extra data or notes that you couldn't complete during the session. Consider the following question for each student.

Did this student successfully make follow-up comments that were appropriate?

Week 6
Keep on Talking!

Background

This week students will use the skills they have learned in Weeks 1 to 5 in longer conversations on a variety of topics. For the most part, topics will be provided for the students so they get practice at talking about a wider variety of interests.

Students will learn that longer conversations consist of the same structure that they have been practicing so far.

Lesson Content

Preparation:

» Set up your space to suit your needs. Ideally you will have a sitting area, a centers area and an active area.
» In your centers area, set up craft, building and board game stations.
» Print the two signs **Ask a Topic-Starter Question** and **Follow-up Comment or Follow-up Question**. These are used as visual prompts if needed.
» Prepare a bowl of conversation topics. See Appendix B.
» Prepare a bowl of conversation parts. See Appendix B.
» You will need one copy of the Week 6 assessment sheet as well as a parent handout for each child.
» Make sure you have a snack ready to serve, but keep it out of view until snack time.

Settle in: 5 Minutes

Probe: Multi-step conversation starting with a topic-starter question

As students arrive, greet them and wait. After a second or two, show them your **Ask a Topic-Starter Question** sign. Once they ask a question, answer it and then see if they do a comment and follow-up. If they do not, show them your second sign.

When the interaction is finished, direct the student to the centers area.

Warm up Activity: 5 minutes

After all the students have arrived, gather them quickly into a fun active game. Remember to keep it simple because you want this activity to last no more than 5 minutes.

Social Skills Topic: 20 minutes

After no more than five minutes of the active game, direct everyone to the seating area. Welcome them back. As usual, get started fast.

> *Hey everyone, welcome back to our social group. We will do our learning and role-play now for about 15 minutes. After that, we will play some more games.*

6.1 Demonstrate the flexibility of conversation

Review the conversation diagram from last week, noting all the pieces that the students know: topic-starter questions, comments, follow-up questions and follow-up comments. Also introduce the idea that conversation is flexible and all the pieces can occur in different orders.

> *Do you remember this diagram from last time?*

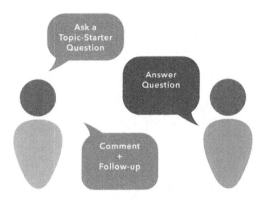

> *We now know all the pieces! Let's look at them. Can anyone tell me what a topic-starter question is?*

» Wait for student response.

> *Yes. It's a question you ask to get a conversation going. It should be about something your friend is interested and about something recent.*
>
> *What about a follow-up question? What is that?*

» Wait for student response.

> *Yes. A follow-up question is when you ask a question that is related to what the person just said.*
>
> *Now, what is a follow-up comment?*

» Wait for student response.

> *Yes. A follow-up comment is when you add new information about what you are talking about.*

» Point to the diagram.

> *On this diagram we have all these pieces happening in a specific order. But a conversation can be more flexible than that.*

» Point to the second person in the diagram.

> *This person can also ask a follow-up question. And then the person he is talking to would answer that question. They could stop there, or add a follow-up.*
>
> *Basically, as long as you are staying on topic, you can add a follow-up question or comment whenever it is your turn and you have answered any questions.*

» Do a rough drawing on the board that has the second person adding a follow-up question instead of just answering the question. Then have the first person answering that question and adding a follow-up question.

> *Let's try a conversation that looks like that. Kelly, can you stand up and talk with me? I'll start.*

» Point to the first speech bubble of your drawing and ask a topic-starter question.

» Point to the second speech bubble and prompt Kelly to answer the question and ask a follow-up question.

» Point to the third speech bubble and answer the question.

> *Excellent! Thanks Kelly.*
>
> *Conversation consists of questions, answers and follow-ups. They are all related to each other and you don't have to worry too much about what order they come in. We're going to practice this today.*

» Pick a card that has a fairly easy topic from the topic bowl.

Peter and Joe, I'd like you to stand up. Peter, I'd like you to ask Joe a question about this topic.

» Show Peter the card you picked.

Joe, answer the question and then both of you continue for a few turns.

As the students talk, comment positively on what you are hearing.

Excellent follow-up question.

Nice follow-up comment.

Good job staying on topic.

If more prompting is needed, say something specific like:

Joe, can you answer Kelly's question?

Kelly, can you comment on Joe's answer?

Joe, can you make a follow-up comment?

Kelly, can you ask a follow-up question?

Prompt students until they have completed a multi-part conversation, with at least three turns per person.

Wow, fantastic! You just had a long conversation! And you used all the conversation pieces we've learned.

Select two more students and give them a topic. Support them through a multi-turn conversation.

Practice Activity: 15 minutes

This activity gives students more highly-supported practice at demonstrating the new skill. This is an important step towards getting them to independently use the skill during the more natural game-based activities in the remainder of the session.

> *Fantastic work everyone! Next I'd like you to all stand up. I am going to put you into pairs for you to have a long conversation. You will pick your topic from the bowl. Try and keep talking on the topic for at least 3 or 4 turns each. If you can go longer, fantastic!*

Put students in pairs and get them started.

Support students through the process. Get them to swap roles when they are done. If there is time, change pairs and redo.

While you are observing, note what problems the students are having. If you see a common thread, like having trouble with making relevant follow-up comments, save a few minutes at the end for some education and practice on the specific skill that is needed.

Watch out for students trying to police the conversation with comments like "S*he was supposed to do a follow-up question.*" In this case, remind the students that conversations flow in different ways. As long as the conversation can continue, there is no problem.

When the time is up:

> *Awesome job! Guess what is next...? Yes, snack!*
>
> *During snack I would like you to talk to each other. If you are stuck for a topic, then just grab one from the bowl.*
>
> *Let's go!*

Snack Break: 20 minutes

Get snack started. Quickly mark the assessment sheet for the previous activity. You will note whether each student needed no support, some support or a lot of support to complete the activity.

During the snack break, if the students talk to each other, stay in the background. If there is no talking, or if one or two students are not talking, prompt the conversation in the usual way.

Game Activity: 20 minutes

If you have access to a gaming system like a Wii-U or even an iPad, feel free to substitute the board game activity with a video game. Make sure it is age-appropriate and one where game turns are relatively short.

Children spend a lot of time playing video games so it is a good environment to practice conversation skills. Players are unlikely to be able to engage in extensive conversation, but you can prompt watchers to comment positively on the player's actions, ask and negotiate turns appropriately, and make conversation (usually game-related) with other non-players.

If you do not have access to a video a game, follow instructions from previous weeks for playing a board game.

Game Show: 20 minutes

In the game show you will practice a variety of skills: topic-starter questions, comments, follow-up comments, follow-up questions.

Begin the game show in the usual way by handing out the buzzers and establishing the rules.

For your questions, choose a topic from the Topics bowl. Then choose a conversation part from the other bowl. So, if you choose **Pokémon Go** and **Follow-up Comment**, your game show question would be:

> *Who can make a follow-up comment about Pokémon Go?*

Return the conversation part to the bowl so it can be chosen again. Alternatively, replace pieces only when the bowl is empty.

Final Group Activity: 15 Minutes

This week, you will give students a bit more practice on talking on a variety of topics. Follow the instructions for this week's practice activity and get students doing multi-turn conversations on a topic they have picked from the bowl.

As parents start to arrive, direct everyone to the centers area.

> *Fantastic job, everyone! Head over to the centers area and keep talking to your buddy.*
>
> *If you need a new topic, just grab one from the bowl.*

Parent Debrief: 10 minutes

As usual, the information for the parent debrief is in the parent handout for this week.

Post Session

Take 5 minutes to review your assessment, adding in any extra data or notes that you couldn't complete during the session. Consider the following questions for each student.

> Did this student successfully participate in a multi-turn conversation without prompting?
>
> Did this student show variety in their conversations? (Sometimes using follow-up comments, sometimes using follow-up questions.)

Week 6 Review

At this point in the course, it is a good idea to review how your students are progressing. If your students are quickly picking up the conversation skills, continue on to Lesson 7. If your students are still awkward with the new skills, make frequent mistakes or fail to use the skills without prompting, then you should consider repeating Lessons 1-6. Use both your knowledge of the student and the parent homework notes to inform your decision.

Repeating the lessons gives lagging students the chance to feel successful as they work again on the foundation skills developed during the first six weeks. It is more important that they develop strong basic conversation skills than complete all the lessons of the course.

If you choose to repeat the lessons, don't make it a penalty or punishment. Instead, frame it as a review that is a natural part of the course. Imply that it is a chance for them to demonstrate their knowledge and skills. You will be able to move more quickly through the material, allowing more time for practice.

There is a letter in Appendix A that you can use to communicate your plans to the parents.

Week 7
Following the Topic

Background

During the last 6 weeks, your students learned the core components of talking with friends: asking appropriate questions, and using follow-up comments and follow-up questions. The remainder of this course focuses on practicing these skills and gradually extending them further.

This week focuses on adapting to the topics our friends are interested in. Often children with ASD have preferred topics and will stick with them, regardless of their friend's response. In this lesson, your students will learn to how to identify conversation clues that indicate what their friend wants to talk about. Your students will also learn how to stay on stay on topic without deviating back to his or her preferred topic.

Lesson Content

Preparation:

> » Set up your space to suit your needs.
> » Print out the Ask me a Topic-Starter Question sign.
> » Print out Question #1 and #2 from Appendix B Week 7 materials.
> » Print out the Conversation Clues statements from Appendix B.
> » Print out the Game Show questions from Appendix B.
> » Print one copy of the Week 7 assessment sheet as well as a parent handout for each child.

» Make sure you have a snack ready to serve, but keep it out of view until snack time.

Settle in: 5 Minutes

Probe: Multi-turn conversation

As students arrive, greet them and pause with an expectant look. You want them to greet you and ask you a topic-starter question. If necessary, hold up your visual prompt.

Once the student has initiated conversation, continue for several turns. Then redirect the student to the centers area.

You may need other students to wait their turn by the door while you complete each brief conversation.

Warm up Activity: 5 minutes

After all the students have arrived, gather them quickly into a fun active game. Feel free to introduce a new game or make a variation of a known game.

As an alternative, you could now designate this time as catch-up time where students talk to each other, using topic-starter questions to ask about each other's recent activities.

If your students need the active time in order to settle for the lesson, keep with the active game. If your students don't need the active activity, try switching to the catch-up time. You could alternate the two options from week to week.

Social Skills Topic: 20 minutes

After no more than five minutes of the active game, direct everyone to the seating area. Welcome them back. As usual, get started fast.

Hey, everyone, welcome back to our social group. We will do our learning and role-play now for about 15 minutes. After that, we will play some more games.

7.1 Acknowledge special interests and their dominance

In this section you help students think about what their special interest is and how it takes up a lot of their thinking time. Sometimes thinking about your own special interest a lot means you miss clues from your friend about what they want to talk about.

> *You all did a fantastic job talking with me when you arrived. Well done! Next time when you arrive, I'd like you to talk to me in the same way. My goal is that I won't need to use my sign to remind you!*
>
> *Today we are going to become topic detectives. Did you know that people we talk with often give us big clues about things they want to talk about? But sometimes we don't notice the clues because are too busy thinking about our own topics.*
>
> *Does anyone here have a special topic that they like to talk about A LOT?*

» Wait for student response. If students are not self-aware, you may need to point out the student's special interest. Make sure you do it in a non-judgmental manner.

> *Hey, Joe. I've noticed that one of your special interests is food. You love thinking about and talking about food, right? Yeah. I love food, too.*
>
> *And Kelly, you love watching Monster High and you like to talk about that a lot, too, right?*
>
> *You both have great special interests. But you know, sometimes, I think you miss some conversation clues because you are still thinking about and talking about your special interest. We all do it sometimes!*
>
> *Today we are going to practice looking for clues about what your friend wants to talk about. It is probably NOT the same thing you want to talk about. But we show we are a friend by talking about what our friend wants to talk about.*
>
> *Let's start looking for clues!*

7.2 Noticing clues

In this section you give students examples of conversation clues that show what our friend wants to talk about. You also demonstrate to the students how to keep on their friend's topic and not convert the topic towards their own special interest.

> *I know that all of you are great at noticing some conversation clues. Today we are going to become even better.*
>
> *Let's start easy. Listen to what I say, then tell me what topic I want to talk about.*
>
> *Hey everyone, I went to Playland this weekend!*

» Pause and then say:

> *Okay, what do I want to talk about?*

» Wait for student response.

> *Yes, I want to talk about Playland. How did you know that?*

» Wait for student response.

> *Yes. Because I told you that I went there and I sounded excited.*

» Hand Question #1 to Peter.

> *Okay, Peter, please ask me this question.*

» Wait for Peter to ask you: What level are you up to in Geometry Dash?

Answer: I don't play Geometry Dash much. I've been playing Soda Dungeon. It's awesome.

» Pause and then say:

Okay, when Peter asks a follow-up question. What topic should it be about?

» Wait for student response.

Yes. It should be about Soda Dungeon. Why?

» Wait for student response.

Yes, because it is something new I am interested in.

Should Peter keep talking about Geometry Dash?

» Wait for student response.

No. Because I have already told you that I am not playing it much. That shows I am not very interested in it.

So, you need to listen to your friend. If they give you a clue that they are not interested in something, then they probably don't want to talk about it.

What they say will give you a clue about what they DO want to talk about.

Now, it's also important that you don't bring your special interest into every topic.

» Give Lisa Question #2.

> *Lisa, ask me this question.*

» Wait for Lisa to ask you: What did you see in Seattle when you visited?

> *Answer: We caught a train about three times and then got on a double-decker bus and we went on a boat with 37 seats.*

» Stop and look at the class.

> *Okay, what did Lisa ask me about?*

» Wait for student response.

> *She asked me what famous sights I saw in Seattle.*
>
> *What did I tell her about?*

» Wait for student response.

> *I told her all about the public transit we caught. Did I answer Lisa's question, or did I think about my own special interest in buses and trains?*

» Wait for student response.

> *Yeah. I didn't really stay on her topic. I talked about MY interests instead, even though I was still talking about Seattle.*
>
> *Why is that a problem?*

» Wait for student response.

> *Lisa didn't ask about busses and trains in Seattle. She asked what famous sights I saw.*
>
> *How do you think she felt when I traded her topic into my own topic?*

» Wait for student response or Lisa's response.

> *Yeah. It makes her feel like I wasn't listening to her. That's not nice.*
>
> *Okay, Lisa, ask me the question again.*

» Wait for Lisa to ask the Seattle question again.

> *I had a great time. We went to the Space Needle, the aquarium and the music museum.*
>
> *All right. How was that answer?*

» Wait for student response.

> *Yeah. I answered her question and stayed on HER topic. I was a good detective. I figured out her topic and stuck to it.*
>
> *Okay, let's do some practice.*

7.3 Role-play

In this section you give students practice at interpreting conversation clues to know what topic to talk about.

> *I am going to say something to each of you. After you answer, we will decide if you stayed with my topic.*

Choose from the following examples. Make sure the student does an initial comment and a follow-up question/comment.

> *My mom won't let me watch Monster High anymore.*
>
> *I went and saw the new superhero movie on the weekend.*
>
> *My dad took me fishing for the first time.*
>
> *Can you believe the Blue Jays lost!*
>
> *My little sister ate a worm.*

After each response, review whether the student stayed with the initial speaker's topic.

Practice Activity: 10 minutes

This activity gives students more highly-supported practice at demonstrating the new skill. This is an important step towards getting them to independently use the skill during the more natural game-based activities in the remainder of the session.

> *Great job, everyone! Now let's practice some more. I'm going to watch and see how you do at following each other's topics. You can choose your own topic, or grab one from the bowl.*

Put the students into pairs and get them talking. Monitor and explain if a student does not follow a topic clue or if he/she morphs the topic to his/her special interest.

Incorporating a special interest is a tricky one. Sometimes it is okay. Sometimes it isn't. Practice and awareness will improve your student's skill at this.

Awesome job! Guess what is next...? Yes, snack!

During snack I would like you to talk to each other. Remember, listen to what your friend is saying to keep track of where the topic is going.

Snack Break: 15 minutes

Get snack started. Then briefly mark the assessment sheet for the previous activity. You will note whether each student needed no support, some support or a lot of support to stay on topic.

During the snack break, if the students talk to each other, stay in the background. If there is no talking, or if one or two students are not talking, prompt the conversation.

Make sure to praise a student if they successfully follow their friend's topic clues.

Board Game Activity: 20 minutes

Initiate your board game as usual, or feel free to introduce new types of games such as card games, Pokémon, etc. You want your students to develop confidence with a wide variety of typical activities.

Game Show: 20 minutes

This week's game show practices following the topic. The game show environment encourages quick thinking which will help promote fluency.

Use the Topic Scenarios from Appendix B Week 7. Read the scenario and then ask *"Did the listener follow the topic clues?"*

After a correct response, ask *"How did you figure that out?"*

After an incorrect response, guide the student through the thinking process to arrive at the correct answer.

When the time is up, finish the game show and move on to the next activity.

Final Group Activity: 15 Minutes

Depending on the energy of your group, decide whether they will do a board game, card game, craft activity, building activity or an active game. Once you have decided on the type of game, give them a choice of three and get them to decide amongst themselves.

As parents start to arrive, finish up the activity.

Parent Debrief: 10 minutes

Debrief the parents as usual, using this week's parent handout.

Post Session

Take 5 minutes to review your assessment, adding in any extra data or notes that you couldn't complete during the session. Consider the following questions for each student.

> Did this student successfully follow the topic?
>
> Did this student avoid morphing the topic to his/her own special interest?

Week 8
Changing Topics

Background

This week students learn how to appropriately change topics. This is a difficult skill for many children, with or without ASD.

Our previous lesson on following the topic was to help children follow the unplanned routes that conversations often take. It helped our students not stay stuck on the same topic and to avoid making every conversation about their own special interest. This week's lesson guides students in how to introduce a new topic into conversation without dropping it in like a bomb.

Students will learn three rules about topic changing.

- You must be part of the conversation before you can change the topic.
- You must choose a topic that interests your friend.
- You only change topic when there is a gap.

Depending on your students, you may need two weeks to successfully introduce and practice these skills. As always, match your session to your students' needs. Repeating a week can allow shaky skills to strengthen.

Lesson Content

Preparation:

» Set up your space to suit your needs.

» Prepare a bowl of topic cards from Appendix B.

» Make sure you have a snack ready to serve, but keep it out of view until snack time.

» You will need a copy of the Week 8 assessment sheet as well as a parent handout for each child.

Settle in: 5 Minutes

Probe: Appropriate follow-up question that attends to topic clues.

As students arrive, greet them and make a comment that gives them a choice of topics for the follow-up question. For example:

> *Hey Joe. I didn't play Minecraft this weekend. I tried out a new game.*

The ideal response would follow up about the new game and not take up the topic of Minecraft. Though be sure to use your own best judgement. Asking why you didn't play Minecraft would be a reasonable follow-up question.

When you have completed a brief conversation with each student, direct them to the centers area.

Warm up / Catch-up Activity: 5 minutes

Choose whether to play an active game or have five minutes of catch-up conversation. See Week 7 for help in making this decision.

Social Skills Topic: 20 minutes

After no more than five minutes, direct everyone to the seating area. Welcome them back. As usual, get started fast.

Hey, everyone, welcome back to our social group. We will do our learning and role-play now for about 15 minutes. After that, we will play some more games.

8.1 Introduce today's subject

Introduce the idea that conversations may cover several topics.

Hey, everyone, when you are having a conversation with someone, do you talk about just one thing, or can your conversation cover several topics?

» Wait for student response.

Yeah. Usually conversations start on one topic and then gradually flow into another topic and then another one. Sometimes, we might think of something related and explicitly change the topic to that.

Today we are going to learn some rules about changing the topic. If you don't follow these rules, your friends might think you are a bit rude.

8.2 Introduce Rule 1: Be a part of the conversation first

Children with ASD are often physically present for a conversation but not paying attention to it. They are then prone to launching into their own topic as soon as there is a chance. This first rule of topic-changing helps children understand that they need to participate in a conversation before they can choose the direction of the conversation.

Our first rule is that you can't change a topic unless you are part of the conversation.

» Write on the whiteboard: 1. Be a part of the conversation before you change the topic.

What do you think Being a part of the conversation means?

» Wait for various student responses.

Yes. Being a part of the conversation means you are listening and talking about the current topic.

Let's see what that looks like.

Kelly and Peter, come up here. Kelly, can you please start a conversation about hiking.

Step up and join the conversation so the three of you are talking. At an appropriate time, make a small topic change to something new. After a few turns on the new topic, stop the conversation.

Thanks Kelly and Peter. Nice job. You can take a seat now.

All right. What was the first topic in the conversation?

» Wait for student response.

Yes, we talked about hiking. What was the second topic of the conversation?

Yes, we talked about other things to do on the weekend. I changed the topic.

Did I meet the rule about being a part of the conversation?

» Wait for student response.

Yes. I participated in the conversation before I changed the topic. My body was oriented to the group. You could tell I was listening because my comments were appropriate. And I talked about the topic.

Now let's see what it looks like if I don't follow the rule.

Call up two more students. This time, do not participate in the conversation. Look around so it is clear you are not paying attention. At an awkward time, abruptly change the topic to something completely different.

Ask the two students in the conversation what that felt like.

After eliciting their feelings:

> *It doesn't feel good if someone just changes the topic if they are not part of the conversation. It makes it feel like they don't care about you because they didn't care enough to listen to what you were talking about.*
>
> *So, what is our first rule about changing topics?*

» Wait for student response.

> *Yes. You have to be a part of the conversation before you can change the topic.*

8.3 Introduce Rule 2: The new topic must be interesting to your friend

The purpose of this rule is to reinforce – yet again – that you need to talk about topics that are interesting to your friend.

> *Now, let's look at our second rule.*

» Write the rule on the board: 2. Choose a topic that is interesting to your friend.

> *This one is a no-brainer. You should talk about things that you and your friends find interesting. We've already talked a lot about that in previous weeks.*

What happens if you choose a topic that only YOU find interesting?

» Wait for student response.

Yeah. Your friends will get bored. Do you want to talk to someone if they only want to talk about their topics? No!

In order to make and keep friends, you need to talk about things your friends are interested in.

So what is our second rule for changing topics?

» Wait for student response.

Yes. The new topic must be interesting to your friend.

8.4 Introduce Rule 3: Change topic when there is a gap

The purpose of this rule is to help your students choose an appropriate time to change the topic. This rule will likely be easy for your students to grasp, but difficult to implement appropriately.

Okay. Third rule!

» Write on the board: 3. Change topic when there is a gap.

The third rule is to change topic when there is a gap. This means that you have to wait for space in the conversation. When you first start talking about a topic there are usually lots of questions and lots of information being traded. Then after a while, you'll find you've covered the important parts of that topic. In that case, when you get a turn to talk, you can change the topic.

Let me show you what that looks like.

Select a student and begin a conversation. At an appropriate gap, change the topic.

At the end, thank the student and ask him to sit down.

That conversation went pretty smoothly. We started talking about camping and then we moved on to talking about skateboarding.

Let's see an example where I don't wait for the gap.

Select a student and begin a conversation. Early in the conversation abruptly change to a new topic.

Thank the student and ask him to sit down.

Well. What happened in that conversation?

» Wait for student response.

Yeah. We had just started on a topic and I changed it too early. I didn't wait for a gap.

Joe, how did it feel when I changed the topic on you?

» Wait for student response.

Yeah. It's a bit confusing. And it made you feel like I am not interested in what you are saying because I didn't follow-up on what you said.

Now, you have to pay attention to a conversation in order to know when there is a gap. You have to wait until everyone has talked about that topic for a while. You have to look at their body language to see if they look like they still want to talk about that topic. It's pretty difficult. Sometimes, you have to wait until everyone actually stops talking for a few seconds. That can be a good clue.

But don't worry, we will practice looking for gaps.

Let's start now. Peter and Lisa, can you stand up please. I am going to give you each a topic.

» Give each student a topic from the bowl of topics.

Peter, please start a conversation on your topic. Lisa, please change the conversation to your topic when you can.

Support your students through the conversation. Give all students a chance to be the topic-changers.

Note to Coach

Students may also need help in prefacing their topic change with appropriate clue words such as:

Hey, that reminds me...

Speaking of camping, I went to the camping store last weekend.

Practice Activity: 10 minutes

This activity gives students more highly-supported practice at demonstrating the new skill. This is an important step towards getting them to independently use the skill during the more natural game-based activities in the remainder of the session.

> *Great job everyone! Now we are going to practice talking with each other and changing topics.*
>
> *But first, let's remind ourselves about the three rules of changing topics.*

» Prompt as needed for students to remember the three rules.

> *Right, now we are ready to have our conversation. You can choose your own topic or grab one from the bowl.*

» Set up your students into groups of two or three. Make sure you are free to supervise.

> *Everybody ready? I'm going to start the conversation, but then I won't be a part of it.*

Start the conversation on one of the topics. Then step away from the group so that you are obviously not part of the group.

Prompt as needed to ensure success. Take note of any common errors that students are making.

Once everyone has changed the conversation to their topic, tell the students that they need to say goodbye to each other as if they were each going to a different class.

> *Awesome job! Take a seat and let's do a quick review.*

Comment on things that students did well and do a quick revision of any areas where students needed a lot of prompting.

> *Guess what is next...? Yes, snack!*
>
> *During snack I would like you to talk to each other. If you are stuck for a topic, then just grab one from the bowl. And remember your three rules when it is time for a topic change.*
>
> *Let's go!*

Snack Break: 15 minutes

Get snack started. Then briefly mark the assessment sheet for the previous activity. You will note whether each student needed no support, some support or a lot of support to complete the activity.

During the snack break, if the students talk to each other, stay in the background. If there is no talking, prompt conversation.

Observe topic changes and prompt for success.

Board Game Activity: 20 minutes

Choose a board game, card game or any activity which you know is a favorite with your students. Ideally it will be a sedentary game rather than active so that conversation is more feasible.

Prompt for conversation and topic changes during the game. Go so far as to instruct a student that it is their turn to change the topic next.

Towards the end, fill in the assessment sheet for this activity. You will note the level of support the student needed to play the game: no support, some support or lots of support. You will also note if each student successfully changed topic based on your explicit prompt or if they changed topic without prompting.

Game Show: 20 minutes

Get the game show organized.

This week you will choose game show questions from a previous week. Review your assessment sheets to find a week where your students found the game show challenging. Use the game show to provide more practice at that skill.

Final Group Activity: 15 Minutes

Depending on the energy of your group, decide whether they will do a board game, craft activity, building activity or an active game. Once you have decided on the type of game, give them a choice of three and get them to decide amongst themselves.

Parent Debrief: 10 minutes

Complete the parent debrief as usual.

Post Session

Take 5 minutes to review your assessment, adding in any extra data or notes that you couldn't do during the session. Consider the following question for each student:

> Did this student successfully change the topic to one of his/her own choosing during a conversation without prompting?

Week 9
Using Eyes & Body to Communicate

Background

This week students learn how to show their friends that they are interested in what they are saying by using appropriate body language and eye contact.

You will know already if your students need practice in these skills. If your students are already skilled in producing appropriate body orientation and eye contact, feel free to skip through the material quickly and instead of doing practice for these two skills, practice multi-turn conversations instead.

If your practice goal becomes multi-turn conversations, begin by requesting students to initiate topics of shared interest. Later on, introduce the bowl of topics. Making conversation on less familiar topics is excellent practice.

Lesson Content

Preparation:

» Set up your space to suit your needs.
» Prepare a bowl of topic cards using the materials in Appendix B.
» Prepare your list of gameshow questions from Appendix B.

» Print the following sign: **Ask Me a Topic-Starter Question**.

» You will need a copy of the Week 9 assessment sheet as well as a parent handout for each child.

» Make sure you have a snack ready to serve, but keep it out of view until snack time.

Settle in: 5 Minutes

Probe: Multi-turn conversation initiated by student.

As students arrive, greet them and pause, but keep looking at them. If they do not ask a topic-starter sentence, show them your sign. Prompt them through a multi-turn conversation.

Let the parents know what time to return.

Warm up Activity: 5 minutes

Choose an active game or do 'catch-up' conversation.

Social Skills Topic: 20 minutes

After no more than five minutes of active game, direct everyone to the seating area. Welcome them back. As usual, get started fast.

> *Hey, everyone, welcome back to our social group. We will do our learning and role-play now for about 15 minutes. After that, we will play some more games.*

9.1 Demonstrate what body orientation communicates.

Students may not be aware that their body language communicates information to their friends.

> *Peter, please stand up, come over here and tell me about your weekend.*

» Wait for Peter to follow your instructions. A few seconds after he begins talking, turn your body away and take a step away.

» Wait a few seconds and turn back. Put your hand up to indicate to Peter to stop talking - if he hasn't already.

Hmmm. What was odd about what I did?

» Wait for student response.

Yes. I turned my body away from Peter when he was talking to me.

Peter, how did that make you feel? What did you think when I turned away?

Wait for Peter's response. You want him to indicate that it was a negative experience for him. If he didn't experience it as negative, seek information from the other students. Your 'turn away' action may not have meaning for Peter.

Hey everyone, what did you think when I turned away while Peter was talking?

If needed, direct students to observations like: You didn't seem interested in what he was saying.

Yes, in our culture, turning away while someone is talking is rude. We need to use our bodies to show we are interested in our friends. We do that by facing our body, or at least our face, towards our friend.

Do we need to do that all of the time or some of the time?

» Wait for student response.

Yeah, we pretty much need to do it all of the time.

If you turn away, what is your friend going to think?

» Wait for student response.

Yes. Your friend will think you are not interested in them. Why is that bad?

» Wait for student response.

If your friend thinks you are not interested in him, that will make him feel bad. If he feels bad, he won't want to hang out with you.

If you want someone to hang out with, you have to always SHOW you are interested when they talk to you.

9.2 Demonstrate what eye contact communicates

Do a similar demonstration for eye contact, showing how it indicates that we are interested in what our friend is saying.

Can anyone suggest how else we can show with our body that we are interested in what our friend is saying?

» Wait for student response.

» If no one guesses eye contact, do the following.

Lisa, can you stand up and ask me about my weekend?

» Wait for Lisa to follow your instructions. When she begins talking to you, look away from her, but make sure your body and face are mostly oriented toward her.

» Answer her without looking at her. Thank her and ask her to sit down.

Okay, Lisa. How did you feel when you talked to me?

Wait for student response. If Lisa was unaware of your lack of eye contact, seek input from the other students. If necessary, replay and hint that students should pay attention to your face.

Yes, I didn't look at her while we were talking. Problem! In our culture it is important to look at people occasionally when we are talking to them. If we don't look, our friend will think we are not interested.

And what happens if our friend thinks we are not interested?

» Wait for student response.

Yeah. They'll go and talk to someone who IS interested. They'll become friends with THEM instead of you.

So, while you are talking with a friend, your job is to make sure you are showing them that you are interested. And how do you show you are interested?

» Wait for student response.

Yes, you show with your body and with your eyes.

9.3 Role-play

The role-play practice ensures all students have a chance to demonstrate good eye contact and body orientation.

> *Let's practice.*
>
> *Kelly and Joe, let's have you stand up here. Kelly, I'd like you to ask Joe a topic-starter question to begin a conversation. Keep talking with each other for a few turns.*
>
> *I'll prompt each of you if you need to pay attention to how your eyes or body are showing your interest.*

Prompt as needed for good eye contact and body orientation. Be vigilant so that students get a good understanding for how much eye contact they need to do.

Repeat with other students until everyone has had a turn.

> *Great job everyone!*

Practice Activity: 10 minutes

This activity gives students more highly-supported practice at eye contact and body orientation. In this activity students will be doing an activity as well as talking. This adds complexity to how much body orientation and eye contact is needed.

> *All right. We are going to build a Lego tower in groups of two. While you are building you need to talk about what you did last weekend. I will be watching and prompting for good body orientation and eye contact.*

Get students organized with the Lego or equivalent building or craft activity. Prompt as needed to guide appropriate body orientation and eye contact.

Switch up the pairs after a while. Feel free to introduce the bowl of topics. This is useful for helping students talk on a wide variety of topics.

Also feel free to vary the activity as different activities need differing amounts of eye contact. Even walking together has different eye contact requirements compared to standing and talking to each other. Give your students a wide variety of scenarios to practice in.

As your time runs out...

> *Great job, everyone.*
>
> *Guess what is next...? Yes, snack!*
>
> *During snack I would like you to talk to each other. If you are stuck for a topic, then just grab one from the bowl. Don't forget what you need to do with your eyes and body.*

Snack Break: 15 minutes

Get snack started. Then briefly mark the assessment sheet for the previous activity. You will note whether each student needed no support, some support or a lot of support to complete the activity.

During the snack break, if the students talk to each other, stay in the background. If there is no talking, or if one or two students are not talking, prompt the conversation.

Pay attention to your students' body orientation and eye contact and prompt as needed.

Board Game Activity: 20 minutes

By now you should have played a variety of board games and even introduced a card game. Try to introduce a new game every two or three weeks for the remainder of the course.

Follow the same procedures in previous weeks to ensure conversation and fun game play.

Prompt for appropriate body orientation/eye contact during the game.

Game Show: 20 minutes

This week choose game show questions from a previous week. Review your assessment sheets to find a week where your students found the game show challenging. Use the game show to provide more practice at that skill.

Final Group Activity: 15 Minutes

Depending on the energy of your group, decide whether they will do a board game, craft activity, building activity or an active game. Once you have decided on the type of game, give them a choice of three and get them to decide amongst themselves.

Parent Debrief: 10 minutes

Conduct your parent debrief as usual.

Post Session

Take 5 minutes to review your assessment, adding in any extra data or notes that you couldn't complete during the session. Consider the following question for each student:

> Is your student using good body orientation and eye contact without prompting?

Week 10 Filtering Comments

Background

This week your students learn to filter their thoughts before saying them.

All children need to learn to filter what they are thinking to avoid making rude or awkward comments. Children with ASD often need extra support in learning this skill.

Lesson Content

Preparation:

> » Set up your space to suit your needs.
> » Print out the Ask Me a Topic-Starter Question sign.
> » Print out the picture of a brain from Appendix D.
> » Print and cut up the Filter Scenarios from Appendix B and place in a bowl.
> » Print one copy of the Week 10 assessment sheet as well as a parent handout for each child.
> » Make sure you have a snack ready to serve, but keep it out of view until snack time.

Settle in: 5 Minutes

Probe: Eye contact and body orientation.

As students arrive, greet them and direct them to the centers area. Compliment or prompt them on the eye contact and body orientation.

Warm up Activity: 5 minutes

Do an active game or 'catch-up' time for five minutes.

Social Skills Topic: 20 minutes

After no more than five minutes of active game, direct everyone to the seating area. Welcome them back. As usual, get started fast.

> *Hey everyone, welcome back to our social group. We will do our learning and role-play now for about 15 minutes. After that, we will play some more games.*

10.1 Introduce the idea of filtering what we say

Show students that if we say whatever is in our head, it can hurt other people's feelings. We need to filter what we say so that we only say nice things.

Most students know what a water filter is, so you can use that as an example of how filtering changes something bad into something good.

> *Does anyone know what a filter is?*

» Wait for student response.

> *Yes, a filter turns something dirty or dangerous into something clean. Often we use a filter to turn dirty water into clean water.*
>
> *Why it is good to turn dirty water into clean water?*

» Wait for student response.

Yes. Because it is better for us.

Today we are going to think about filtering what we say.

Let's think about what goes on in our brains. We have lots of thoughts about lots of different topics.

» Draw a picture of a head with lots of thoughts in it or use the picture of a brain from Appendix D. Give some examples of what your brain might contain.

Now imagine I have a new backpack. I think it's awesome. My friend Liam sees it and he thinks the backpack is ugly. Let's pretend this is Liam and put that thought in his head.

» Put Liam's name above the head. Add the ugly thought to Liam's brain.

What would happen if Liam shared his thought with me?

» Wait for student response.

If he told me the backpack is ugly, that would make me feel bad. What should Liam do instead?

» Wait for student response.

Right. He could say nothing. Or he could say something nice about the backpack.

He should FILTER his thoughts. That means you keep the rude or awkward thoughts in your head. These are the thoughts that are going to make someone feel bad.

The other thoughts you can say.

The filter in our brain acts just like the water filter. It keeps the unpleasant stuff in and lets out the things that are nice to say.

Better still, we can use that filter to CHANGE our thoughts from unpleasant to nice.

10.2 Filter from unpleasant to nice

Give an example of changing a rude thought into a nice comment.

Let's think about my new backpack again. Liam doesn't like it. But he wants to say something nice. What he can do is look at it and find SOMETHING that he thinks is nice. Maybe it is the color, maybe it is the shape, maybe it is the cool water bottle pocket on the side.

To be a good friend, he needs to find something nice he can say.

Peter, what could you say if you were Liam?

» Wait for student response.

Good job.

Let's practice finding something nice to say. We will change our unpleasant thought into a nice comment.

Pick two negative examples from your bowl of Filter Scenarios and work through them with your students.

10.3 It's perfectly fine to have negative thoughts

Some students might worry that it is bad to even think negative thoughts. Reassure your students that we all have all sort of crazy thoughts in our head and that is perfectly okay. We just have to make sure to be careful what comes out of our mouth.

Hey everyone, great job at converting unpleasant or negative thoughts into something nice to say. Now, here's a question. Is it okay to have unpleasant thoughts?

» Wait for student response.

You know what? You might be surprised by this. It is perfectly okay to have unpleasant thoughts. Our brains are full of crazy stuff and we can't always control what we think about. So don't worry about having unpleasant thoughts in your brain.

What you do need to do is make sure that you don't SAY all those things. You need to filter before you say something.

10.4 How to decide if it is okay to say

Your students may be experts at converting their thoughts into something nice to say, but that is no help if they don't know when to apply the skill. In this section you help students identify when they need to filter a thought.

Now, how do you know which thoughts are okay to say and which are not. Any ideas?

» Wait for student response.

Great answers. The easiest way to decide if you should say something is to think about how YOU would feel if someone said it to you. Let's look at some examples.

You are playing a video game and your dad wants to talk to you. You say "Go away" because you want to finish the level.

Now, imagine if you went to your friend's place and knocked on the door. He opens the door and says "Go away" to you. How would you feel?

» Wait for student response.

Yeah. You would feel bad. So how do you think your dad feels when you tell him to go away?

» Wait for student response.

Yeah, he would feel bad. So instead of saying, "Go away", you need to filter that into something nicer. Any ideas for what you could say?

» Wait for student response.

Yeah. You could say, "Hold on, I just need to finish the level," or "Can I finish the level?"

Right. What was our test to decide whether we need to filter our thoughts?

» Wait for student response.

Yeah. We think about how WE would feel if someone said that to us.

Let's practice. Peter and Lisa, please stand up. Peter, choose a scenario from this bowl and read it aloud.

» Wait for Peter to read the filter scenario.

> *Okay. Lisa, what can you say in this situation?*

» Wait for Lisa's response.

> *Great job!*

Switch roles until everyone has had a turn at choosing from the bowl and responding to the scenario.

Practice Activity: 10 minutes

This activity gives students more highly-supported practice at demonstrating the new skill. This is an important step towards getting them to independently use the skill during the more natural game-based activities in the remainder of the session.

> *Great job, everyone! Now let's practice some more.*

Put the students into pairs and get them to take turns at choosing from the bowl. Switch the pairs about half way through.

> *Awesome job! Guess what is next...? Yes, snack!*
>
> *During snack I would like you to talk to each other. Remember, filter any negative*
>
> *thoughts and say something nice.*

Snack Break: 15 minutes

Get snack started. Then briefly mark the assessment sheet for the previous activity. You will note whether each student needed no support, some support or a lot of support to complete the activity.

During the snack break, if the students talk to each other, stay in the background. If there is no talking, or if one or two students are not talking, prompt the conversation.

Board Game Activity: 20 minutes

Initiate your board game as usual, or feel free to introduce new types of games such as card games, Pokémon, etc. You want your students to develop confidence with a wide variety of typical activities.

Game Show: 20 minutes

This week's game show practices filtering comments. The game show environment encourages quick thinking which will help promote fluency.

Use the Filter Scenarios from Appendix B Week 7. Read the scenario and then ask *"Should I filter? Yes or No?"*

After a correct response, ask *"What can I say?"*

When the time is up, finish the game show and move on to the next activity.

Final Group Activity: 15 Minutes

Depending on the energy of your group, decide whether they will do a board game, card game, craft activity, building activity or an active game. Once you have decided on the type of game, give them a choice of three and get them to decide amongst themselves.

Parent Debrief: 10 minutes

Debrief parents as usual.

Post Session

Take 5 minutes to review your assessment, adding in any extra data or notes that you couldn't complete during the session. Consider the following question for each student:

Did this student successfully filter comments when needed?

Week 11
Beginning & Ending a Conversation

Background

Children with ASD sometimes launch into a conversation about their special interest without any greetings or conversation warm ups. Similarly, they may walk away when they are done talking without ending the conversations appropriately.

This week students learn how to begin and end a conversation appropriately.

Lesson Content

Preparation:

> » Set up your space to suit your needs.
> » Print out the conversation diagram, or draw it on the board.
> » Get your bowl of topic cards ready.
> » You will need a copy of the Week 11 assessment sheet as well as a parent handout and final activity info sheet for each child.
> » Make sure you have a snack ready to serve, but keep it out of view until snack time.

Settle in: 5 Minutes

Probe: Appropriate multi-turn conversation.

As students arrive, greet them and step through a brief conversation with them. If another student arrives, incorporate them into the conversation. When appropriate direct the students to the centers area.

Warm up Activity: 5 minutes

Do a five-minute active game or catch-up period.

Social Skills Topic: 20 minutes

After no more than five minutes of active game, direct everyone to the seating area. Welcome them back. As usual, get started fast.

> *Hey everyone, welcome back to our social group. We will do our learning and role-play now for about 15 minutes. After that, we will play some more games.*

11.1 Introduce the revised conversation diagram

Introduced the revised conversation diagram that now shows steps for beginning and ending a conversation. Demonstrate how to begin and end a conversation appropriately.

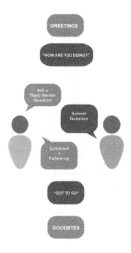

This week we are going to talk about how to begin and end a conversation.

» Point to conversation diagram.

Here's a diagram of how a good conversation works. Let's go through it.

A conversation starts with....

» Wait for student response.

Yes, you start a conversation by saying "Hello" or "Hi." Sometimes just a nod is enough to start a conversation.

And how do you end a conversation?

» Wait for student response.

Yeah. You say "Good bye" or "See you" or "Catch you later." Something that shows that you are done talking for now.

Now, let's look at this step after saying hello. I call it the warm-up step. This is where you ask about the other person to see how they are doing. You could say "How are you doing?" If your friend was sick last time you saw them, you could say "Are you feeling better now?"

So, what do you do in the warm-up step?

» Wait for student response.

Yeah, you ask how the other person is doing.

Now, let's look at the step before you say good-bye. Let's call this the cool-down step. This is where you let the other person know that it's time for you to go. You can say things like:

I've got to go.

Oops. My class starts in 5 minutes.

My mom is expecting me home.

Do you have any other ideas for what you could say to let the other person know that you need to finish the conversation?

» Wait for student response.

Great answers!

Now, let's look at this section. This is the middle of the conversation where all the talking happens. This is where you talk about different topics. You can stay in this section for a while as you talk about a topic for a few turns and then move onto a new topic.

Then when it is time to finish the conversation, you step towards the end. (Point to the relevant bubbles.)

Let's go through the whole picture again. How do we start a conversation?

» Wait for student response.

Yes. We say hello!

What comes next...?

Continue stepping though each part of the conversation diagram.

11.2 When to use all the steps

Make sure that students understand that not all conversations need all the steps. Usually you only do all the beginning steps if you haven't seen your friend for a while. Similarly, you typically only do all the ending steps if you won't see your friend again for a while.

> *Sometimes you don't need to use all these steps. For example, if recess ends and you and your friend are going to the same class, you can just continue your conversation as you go to class.*
>
> *But if your friend was going to go to a different class, you might say "See you later." It all depends when you are going to see your friend again. If you won't see them again that day, you need to make sure you complete all the steps and say goodbye.*
>
> *Let's think about an example. Lisa, you were talking with Peter before class started. When I said it was time to start class, does that mean you need to say goodbye to Peter?*

» Wait for student response.

> *No, you can just do a cool down like "Let's talk more later" or even just smile at him as you turn your attention to me.*
>
> *All right... Let's practice a complete conversation. Joe and Kelly, please stand up. Let's pretend you have both arrived at school at the same time. Please have a conversation that contains each of these steps. I'll help if you forget.*

Prompt Joe and Kelly through each part of the conversation. After a minute or two of conversation, say;

> *Okay, the bell has rung and you need to go to separate classes. You may not see each other for the rest of the day.*

Afterwards, select two more students to have a similar conversation.

Practice Activity: 10 minutes

This activity gives students more highly-supported practice at demonstrating the new skill. This is an important step towards getting them to demonstrate the skill during the more natural game-based activities in the remainder of the session.

> *All right. Let's practice some more conversations. You can talk with your partner about any topic. If you need help thinking about a topic, choose one from the topic bowl before you start.*
>
> *Keep talking with your partner until I clap my hands. When you hear me clap my hands you need to finish up the conversation. You won't see your friend again for a week, so make sure you finish your conversation properly.*
>
> *What do you do when I clap my hands?*

» Wait for student response.

> *Yes. You finish the conversation. How do you finish conversation? Do you just walk away?*

» Wait for student response.

> *Yes. First you cool down the conversation by letting your friend know that you need to finish talking. Then you say goodbye.*

Pair up the students and get them to begin a conversation. Prompt as needed to ensure that all the steps in the conversation diagram are completed appropriately. After students have talked for a few minutes, clap your hands. Prompt the final stages of the conversation diagram as needed.

Switch up the pairs and repeat. If you have the time, get your students to practice a scenario where they will go with their friend to a class. In this case, make sure your students have a more casual conversation transition.

> *Awesome job! Guess what is next...? Yes, snack!*
>
> *During snack I would like you to talk to each other. If you are stuck for a topic, then just grab one from the bowl.*
>
> *Let's go!*

Snack Break: 15 minutes

Get snack started. Then briefly mark the assessment sheet for the previous activity. You will note whether each student needed no support, some support or a lot of support to complete the activity.

Prompt for conversation, as usual. Make sure students don't use any conversation starters or finishers as that is not appropriate now.

Board Game Activity: 20 minutes

Choose a board game, card game or any activity which you know is a favorite with your students. Ideally it will be a sedentary game rather than active so that conversation is more feasible.

Prompt for conversation and comments during the game.

Towards the end, fill in the assessment sheet for this activity. You will note the level of support the student needed to play the game: no support, some support, lots of support. You will also evaluate how each student participated in conversation during the game.

If the game is going well, continue it without comment. If the game is not successful, finish it early.

> *Hey, we have run out of time for this today. Let's pack-up and get on to the game show.*

Game Show: 20 minutes

Get the game show organized.

This week you will choose game show questions from a previous week. Review your assessment sheets to find a week where your students found the game show challenging. Use the game show this week to provide more practice at that skill.

Final Group Activity: 10 Minutes

Depending on the energy of your group, decide whether they will do a board game, craft activity, building activity or an active game. Once you have decided on the type of game, give your students a choice of three and get them to decide amongst themselves.

Your game this week will be a little shorter as you will need to brief your students for the final week activity.

Briefing for Next Week: 5 Minutes

Introduce next week's activity. Depending on your group, you may visit a pizza restaurant, go bowling, etc. Clarify with your students:

Where and when to meet
That they should practice their best conversation skills.
Where and when for parent pickup

Parent Debrief: 10 minutes

Debrief the parents as usual. The information to cover is contained in the parent handout for this week. Make sure to tell the parents about next week's activity.

Post Session

Take 5 minutes to review your assessment, adding in any extra data or notes that you couldn't complete during the session. Consider the following question for each student.

Did this student successfully begin and end a conversation?

Week 12
Pizza Party

Background

This week's goal is for students to practice their conversation skills in a new environment. Your students will have become quite adept at conversation in your learning environment. However, children with ASD often struggle to generalize skills to new environments.

For this week, arrange to meet at a local coffee shop, pizza restaurant or diner. Alternatively, choose an activity like bowling, swimming etc.

The goal is for students to get together and have fun and talk with each other!

Lesson Content

Preparation:

» Make sure you have a booking if you are going to a restaurant or an activity like bowling.
» Print out the Week 12 assessment and final parent handout.
» Print out certificates for each student.
» Complete the Week 12 assessment ahead of time. You will use this information when talking with students and parents after the final session.

At the Location:

Encourage students to greet each other while you confirm pickup time and place with the parents.

Arrange seating so that students can talk together. If you have more than four students, arrange them into two separate groups with you in the middle. In this case, make sure to mix up the groups part way through the session.

Enjoy the food/activity with your students. If conversation lags, prompt a student to begin a topic rather than leaping in yourself.

At some point during the session, hand out the certificates. Make sure to mention a specific, encouraging achievement for each student.

As the session comes to an end, prompt for good conversation finishes with cool-downs and goodbyes.

Parent Debrief: 10 minutes

As parents arrive, thank them for supporting their child so well through the course. For each child, tell the parent about a specific positive change that you have seen. Parents love to hear about genuine progress.

Suggest to parents that they keep prompting and encouraging the new skills to ensure they generalize into everyday situations. The Week 12 handout provides a summary for them to use going forward.

Post Session

Celebrate the successful completion of the course!

Appendix A
Parent Letters

In this section you will find the parent homework sheets for each weekly lesson. You will need to print one copy for each student in the group.

The first week contains additional Parent Debrief Notes for the coach to reference when talking to the parents at the end of the first class.

Parent Debrief Notes

Please cover the following topics in your Week 1 parent debrief.

Drop off

- Parents should bring their child so the child can greet the coach and then the parents should leave quickly. Where possible, questions should be saved until the end.
- Students should arrive on time so the group can get started quickly.
- If the group has started, the coach is unavailable to talk to parents. The parent should make eye contact as their child arrives and then leave.

Pickup

- Tell the parents where to wait when they arrive for pickup. Often it is best if they wait away from the activity area so that children are not distracted. Then, when it is time, go talk to the parents or invite them into the social group space.
- Tell the parents what time to arrive for pickup.

Homework

- Explain that there is weekly homework. Their child will be involved in the homework, but it is the parent's responsibility to complete the homework. You will not ask the children if they have done their homework. You will ask the parents.
- Homework is to be handed in by the parents at the beginning of class. Please save questions/comments for after class.

Support at Home

- Explain that students need as many generalization opportunities as possible in order to make skills automatic. Even beyond the homework, parents should look for opportunities to practice the newly learned skills.
- Parents should support children with prompting as needed. If there is interest from the parents, arrange to photocopy the section on prompting from this manual.

Parent Homework Week 1

Social Skill Topic

This week your child learned how to discover what their friend is interested in. Knowing a friend's interests is the first step in choosing an appropriate conversation topic.

Your child practiced two types of questions.

> What is your favorite _____? e.g. What is your favorite movie?

> What did you do last _____? e.g. What did you do last weekend?

Your goal this week is to give your child opportunities to practice these questions. Please find at least four opportunities where your child can talk with a peer or adult and ask these questions.

The students were also introduced to the following idea.

We talk to friends about SHARED INTERESTS

Your child is now aware of this idea, but we don't expect that they will be able to apply this rule yet. Feel free to gently reinforce this concept when appropriate.

Task 1: Homework Review

Sit down with your child and go over Task 2. Talk about what they need to do to complete the task. Brainstorm together to identify opportunities where the practice could occur. (This part is important as it helps your child realize when these questions can be appropriately used in conversation.) Do a quick role-play with your child to practice the skill.

Task 2: Discover Interests

Talk to four people and find out one interest for each. Participants can be family members, neighbors, teachers, friends, etc.

Where possible, integrate the questions into a natural conversation. i.e. don't let your child just walk away after they have asked the question. Prompt them to continue the conversation for at least a few turns.

At some point after the conversation, fill in the worksheet on the next page with the help of your child. You can do the writing, but make sure your child tells you what to put in each section.

My Name_____

Opportunity 1

I talked to:

I asked them:

I know they are interested in:

because they said:

Opportunity 2

I talked to:

I asked them:

I know they are interested in:

because they said:

Opportunity 3

I talked to:

I asked them:

I know they are interested in:

because they said:

Opportunity 4

I talked to:

I asked them:

I know they are interested in:

because they said:

Task 3: Parent Comments

Please comment on how your child fared when completing Task 2. Did you need to give a high level of prompting, or was the occasional suggestion sufficient? Could your child interpret what they heard to identify their talking partner's interests?

Task 4: Hand in homework

Please hand in the homework to the coach at the beginning of the next social group.

Parent Homework Week 2

Social Skill Topic

This week your child learned how to ask a **topic-starter question**.

A topic-starter question is used to start a conversation with a friend or begin a new topic during a conversation. Students use knowledge about shared interests to ask appropriate topic-starter questions.

Some examples of topic-starter questions are:

> *John, did you play Minecraft this week?*
>
> *Megan, did you go see the Angry Birds movie like you planned?*

Generally, topic-starter questions must be:

- Related to the interests of the friend, not the interests of the speaker. Shared interests are okay.
- About recent activity related to that interest.

Your goal this week is to give your child opportunities to practice using topic-starter questions. Please find at least four opportunities where your child can talk to yourself or another child or adult and ask these questions. Please try for four different individuals.

Task 1: Homework Review

Sit down with your child and go over Task 2. Talk about what activities they need to do to complete the task. Brainstorm together to identify opportunities during the week where the practice could occur. (This part is important as it helps your child realize when these questions can be appropriately used in conversation.)

Ask your child what reminder they would like so they remember what they need to do. We also recommend doing a role-play with you to practice the skill beforehand.

Task 2: Ask Topic-Starter Questions

Ask a topic-starter question to begin a conversation with four different people during the week. Participants can be family members, neighbors, teachers, friends, etc.

Where possible, integrate the questions into a natural conversation. For example, topic-starter questions usually occur after greetings. Also, don't let your child just walk away after they have asked the question. Prompt them to continue the conversation for at least a few turns.

After the conversation, fill in the worksheet on the following page with the help of your child. You can do the writing, but make sure your child tells you what to put in each section.

Opportunity 1:   *I talked to:*

My topic-starter question was:

My question was related to their interests YES / NO

My question asked about recent activity   YES / NO

Opportunity 2:   *I talked to:*

My topic-starter question was:

My question was related to their interests YES / NO

My question asked about recent activity   YES / NO

Opportunity 3:   *I talked to :*

My topic-starter question was:

My question was related to their interests YES / NO

My question asked about recent activity   YES / NO

Opportunity 4:   *I talked to:*

My topic-starter question was:

My question was related to their interests YES / NO

My question asked about recent activity   YES / NO

Task 3: Parent Comments

Please comment on how your child fared when completing Task 2. Did you need to give a high level of prompting, or was the occasional suggestion sufficient? Did your child ask appropriate topic-starter questions?

Task 4: Hand in homework

Please hand in the homework to the coach at the beginning of the next social group.

Parent Homework Week 3

Social Skill Topic

This week your child learned how to make an appropriate comment when their friend says something or does something. A comment is when you say something nice to show you listened.

Your child learned the following rules about comments.

- Comment when your friend does something or says something.
- Match the comment to the information.

e.g. Happy comments for happy information. Sad comments for sad information.

Some examples of appropriate comments are:

A: I went to Playland yesterday!

B: That sounds like fun!

A: My dog died yesterday.

B: I'm sorry. You must feel sad.

Student A throws the basketball through the hoop.

B: Nice shot!

Your goal this week is to give your child many opportunities to practice making comments. Most of this practice can be with you. However, it is always great if you get additional adults involved.

To begin with, you may need to prompt that it is an appropriate time for a comment. Consider using a gestural prompt like your fingers shaped like a C. Teach your child that when you do that sign, you are telling her it is a good time for her to make a comment.

Your goal is for your child to do at least 10 unprompted comments this week. You may need to do dozens of prompted comments before unprompted comments start to come naturally.

Task 1: Homework Review

Sit down with your child and explain the goal for the week: 10 unprompted comments.

Show him the sign you will use as a clue when it is a good time for a comment.

Practice a few comments just to make sure your child understands the goal.

Task 2: Comment Data

On at least four days, put aside five minutes to explicitly practice conversation with your child. Your child does not need to be aware of your goal. Do a rough count of how many prompted and unprompted comments your child produces during the five minutes.

Celebrate your child's success with positive comments.

	Day 1	Day 2	Day 3	Day 4
Prompted Comments (guesstimate)				
Unprompted Comments (guesstimate)				

Task 3: Parent Comments

Please comment on how your child fared at making comments during the week. Did you reach the goal of 10 unprompted comments? All information is useful for the coach to appropriately adapt upcoming lessons.

Task 4: Hand in homework

Please hand in the homework to the coach at the beginning of the next social group.

Parent Homework Week 4

Social Skill Topic

This week your child learned how to ask an appropriate follow-up question when their friend has said something. Your child learned that follow-up questions are related to what the person just said.

Some examples of appropriate follow-up questions are:

A: I went to Playland yesterday!

B: That sounds like fun! What rides did you go on?

A: We went camping on the weekend.

B: Cool. Where did you go?

Follow-up questions are often preceded by a brief comment, as illustrated in the previous examples.

Your goal this week is to prompt your child to ask follow-up questions.

To begin with, you may need to prompt that it is an appropriate time for a follow-up question. Consider using a gestural prompt like making a 'Q' with your fingers. Teach your child that when you do that sign, you are telling her it is a good time for her to ask a follow-up question.

To make the gesture, make a circle with one hand and use your other index finger to tap the circle, forming the cross piece on the 'Q'. Or use any gesture that you both agree means "Ask a follow-up question."

Your goal is for your child to do at least 10 unprompted follow-up questions this week. You may need to do dozens of prompted questions before unprompted follow-up questions start to come naturally.

Task 1: Homework Review

Sit down with your child and explain the goal for the week: 10 unprompted follow-up questions.

Show him the sign you will use as a clue when it is a good time for a follow-up question.

Practice a few follow-up questions just to make sure your child understands the goal.

Task 2: Comment Data

On at least four days, put aside 5 minutes to explicitly practice conversation with your child. Your child does not need to be aware of your goal. Do a rough count of how many prompted and unprompted follow-up questions your child produces during the 5 minutes.

Celebrate your child's success.

	Day 1	Day 2	Day 3	Day 4
Prompted Follow-up Questions (guesstimate)				
Unprompted Follow-up Questions (guesstimate)				

Task 3: Parent Comments

Please comment on how your child fared at asking follow-up questions during the week. Did you reach the goal of 10 unprompted follow-up questions?

All information is useful for the coach to appropriately adapt upcoming lessons.

Task 4: Hand in homework

Please hand in the homework to the coach at the beginning of the next social group.

Parent Homework Week 5

Social Skill Topic

This week your child learned how to make appropriate follow-up comments when their friend has said something.

Follow-up comments add personal information about the speaker that is NEW information and is RELATED to what the person just said.

In the following examples, the follow-up comments are bolded.

> A: I went to Playland yesterday!
>
> B: That sounds like fun! **I went on the weekend, too!**

> A: We had spaghetti for dinner last night.
>
> B: Cool. **We had pizza**.

Follow-up comments are often preceded by a brief comment, as illustrated in the previous examples. Follow-up comments can be used instead of a follow-up question, or as well as a follow-up question.

Your goal this week is to prompt your child to make follow-up comments.

To begin with, you may need to prompt when it is an appropriate time for a follow-up comment. Consider using a gestural prompt like making a 'C' with your fingers. Teach your child that when you do that sign, you are telling her it is a good time for her to ask a follow-up comment.

Your goal is for your child to do at least 10 unprompted follow-up comments this week. You may need to do dozens of prompted comments before unprompted follow-up comments start to come naturally.

Task 1: Homework Review

Sit down with your child and explain the goal for the week: 10 unprompted follow-up comments.

Show him the sign you will use as a clue when it is a good time for a follow-up comment.

Practice a few follow-up comments, making sure your child understands the goal and can demonstrate the skill.

Task 2: Comment Data

On at least four days, put aside 5 minutes to explicitly practice conversation with your child. Your child does not need to be aware of your goal. Do a rough count of how many prompted and unprompted follow-up comments your child produces during the 5 minutes.

Keep in mind that a follow-up comment contains NEW information that is RELATED to what you just said. It is more than just saying 'Cool' or 'That's awesome'.

Celebrate your child's success.

	Day 1	Day 2	Day 3	Day 4
Prompted Follow-up Comments (guesstimate)				
Unprompted Follow-up Comments (guesstimate)				

Task 3: Parent Comments

Please comment on how your child fared at making follow-up comments during the week. Did you reach the goal of 10 unprompted follow-up comments?

All information is useful for the coach to appropriately adapt upcoming lessons.

Task 4: Hand in homework

Please hand in the homework to the coach at the beginning of the next social group.

Parent Homework Week 6

Social Skill Topic

This week your child practiced multi-turn conversations on a variety of topics. They used the following skills developed in previous weeks: asking topic-starter questions, commenting, asking a follow-up question, making a follow-up comment.

Your goal this week is to provide your child with opportunities to participate in multi-turn conversations with you and where possible, with other known people.

Specific details are given in the tasks below.

Task 1: Homework Review

Sit down with your child and explain the goals for the week:

- 10 unprompted topic-starter questions
- 10 unprompted follow-up questions
- 10 unprompted follow-up comments
- Multi-turn conversation on at least 4 different topics

Discuss who your child will talk with and possible topics for each person. (Remember, the ideal topic is a shared interest.)

Task 2: Conversation Data

Setting aside specific time each day to converse is the best way to ensure adequate practice. Complete the following chart after your 'conversation time'.

	Day 1	Day 2	Day 3	Day 4
Topic-Starter questions - unprompted				
Follow-up questions - unprompted				

	Day 1	Day 2	Day 3	Day 4
Follow-up comments - unprompted				

Task 3: Parent Comments

Please comment on how your child fared at making conversation during the week. Did you reach the goals? All information is useful for the coach to appropriately adapt upcoming lessons.

Task 4: Hand in homework

Please hand in the homework to the coach at the beginning of the next social group.

Parent Update

We are halfway through the *How to Talk with Friends* curriculum!

At this point, the curriculum gives us the option of continuing through the remaining lessons or activating a circular learning approach where we focus on reviewing the skills developed in the first part of the course.

After reviewing the skills of your child and the other children in the group, we have decided to implement the circular learning where we revisit the taught skills and provide more practice.

The benefit of this approach is that these skills will become more automatic and part of your child's available repertoire of skills. Without this extra practice, your child will still need prompts to use the skills. They will not be part of your child's available repertoire of skills.

Over the next few weeks, you can look forward to seeing the improvement in your child's skills from when you first practiced each skill in the homework exercises. Please support your child with your enthusiasm and your attention to the homework exercises.

If you have any questions, feel free to contact us or talk to us at the end of the next session.

Parent Homework Week 7

Social Skill Topic

Often children with ASD have preferred topics and will stick with them, regardless of their friend's response.

In this lesson, your child practiced identifying conversation clues that indicate what his/her friends want to talk about. Your child also practiced staying on topic without deviating back to his/her preferred topic.

Task 1: Topic Following Data

At least four times during the week, put aside five minutes for conversation with your child.

While you are conversing with your child, note if they need support to appropriately follow the topic of conversation. Prompt your child if they fail to follow onto a new topic or if they inappropriately attempt to morph the topic into their special interest.

	Day 1	Day 2	Day 3	Day 4
Successfully followed to new topic				
Prompts to follow on to new topic.				
Prompts for inappropriate change to special interest.				

Task 3: Parent Comments

Please comment on how your child fared at following topics. Did your child listen and adjust questions and comments as the topic changed? Did your child stick with the shared topic or did he/she try to inject his/her special interest? All information is useful for the coach to appropriately adapt upcoming lessons.

Task 4: Hand in homework

Please hand in the homework to the coach at the beginning of the next social group.

Parent Homework Week 8

Social Skill Topic

This week your child learned how to change the topic during a conversation. This is an extremely challenging skill. Be prepared for weeks of practice.

Your child learned three guidelines for changing a topic.

- You have to be an active part of a conversation before you can change the topic.
- The new topic must be interesting to your friends.
- You need to wait for a gap in the conversation. This means the current topic is slowing down and everyone is ready for a new topic.

Your goal this week is to give your child practice at appropriately changing topics in a conversation.

Specific details are given in the tasks below.

Task 1: Topic Change Data

At least four times during the week, put aside five minutes for conversation with your child.

While you are conversing with your child, note if they need support to appropriately introduce a new topic

If your child is not changing topics without prompts, prompt your child do so.

	Day 1	Day 2	Day 3	Day 4
Chose new topic that is a shared interest				
Chose good time for topic change				

Note down the total number of times that your child changed the topic and the number of those topic-changes that were prompted. E.g. 5-3 means your child changed the topic 5 times and 3 of those times were prompted.

Task 3: Parent Comments

Please comment on how your child fared at changing topics. Did your child choose appropriate topics? Did your child show good timing in changing the topic? All information is useful for the coach to appropriately adapt upcoming lessons.

Task 4: Hand in homework

Please hand in the homework to the coach at the beginning of the next social group.

Parent Homework Week 9

Social Skill Topic

This week your child learned how to use appropriate body orientation and eye contact to show that they are interested in what their friend is saying.

Your goal this week is to give your child gentle prompts when he/she is not using their body orientation and eye contact to show they are paying attention to you.

Specific details are given in the tasks below.

Task 1: Body Orientation Data

At least four times during the week, set a timer for five minutes and observe the body language and eye contact of your child while you are doing an activity together. Try to choose different activities. For example: at the dinner table, walking together to school, playing a board game, grocery shopping, etc.

During that time, require good body orientation and eye contact. Note how many times you need to prompt for eye contact or body orientation. Make sure you don't require too much eye contact or body orientation. For example, walking and talking requires less eye contact than if you were standing and talking with each other.

	Day 1	Day 2	Day 3	Day 4
Body orientation prompts				
Eye contact prompts				

Note down the number of prompts needed.

Task 2: Parent Comments

Please comment on how your child fared at body orientation/eye contact. Did your child show appropriate body language? All information is useful for the coach to appropriately adapt upcoming lessons.

Task 4: Hand in homework

Please hand in the homework to the coach at the beginning of the next social group.

Parent Homework Week 10

Social Skill Topic

This week your child learned about filtering thoughts before saying something. Your child learned:

- You should filter a thought if you would feel bad if someone said it to you.
- You filter a thought by finding something nice to say instead.

Your goal this week is to cue your child with the word 'filter' on all occasions where a thought should have been filtered. Where possible, also educate other adults in your child's life to use the same terminology.

Specific details are given in the tasks below.

Task 1: Homework Review

Sit down with your child and explain that you will use the word *filter* when he/she should have filtered a thought. When your child hears the word *filter,* he/she need to come up with something nicer to say.

If your child likes to police other children's behavior, you should remind them that it is not their job to tell other children or adults to filter. You can remind your child that you are always happy to discuss with them if they are concerned about another child's behavior.

Task 2: Filter Data

Depending on your child, you may have many opportunities to practice filtering during the week or you may have few opportunities.

If you have few opportunities, feel free to give your child hypothetical scenarios related to their life. For example:

> *You go to Mika's house and her mom serves you <disliked food> for dinner. What could you say?*

Try to do four scenarios per day.

Task 3: Parent Comments

Please comment on how your child fared at filtering during the week. Did you reach the goals? All information is useful for the coach to appropriately adapt upcoming lessons.

Task 4: Hand in homework

Please hand in the homework to the coach at the beginning of the next social group.

Parent Homework Week 11

Social Skill Topic

Often children with ASD will launch into a conversation about their special interest without any greetings or conversation warm ups. Similarly, they may walk away when they are done talking without ending the conversations appropriately.

This week your child practiced beginning and ending conversations. Students learned that a complete conversation has several steps.

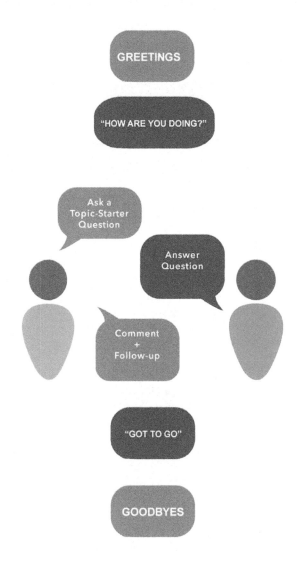

Your goal this week is to give your child practice at completing whole conversations with your and other people in his/her close community.

Specific details are given in the tasks below.

Task 1: Homework Review

Sit down with your child and go over Task 2. Brainstorm together who they can have conversations with. Identify at least 4 people your child can converse with. Participants can be family members, neighbors, teachers, friends, etc.

Make sure the conversation opportunity is natural. Don't do a pretend conversation. It is important that your child practices these skills in real situations.

Task 2: Conversations

At some point after each conversation, fill in this worksheet with the help of your child. You can do the writing, but make sure your child tells you what to put in each section.

Opportunity 1

I talked to:

I completed these steps during my conversation:

__ Greetings   __ "Got to go" warning

__ "How are you doing?"   __ Goodbyes

What I would do better next time:

Opportunity 2

I talked to:

I completed these steps during my conversation:

__ Greetings   __ "Got to go" warning

__ "How are you doing?"   __ Goodbyes

What I would do better next time:

Opportunity 3

I talked to:

I completed these steps during my conversation:

__ Greetings   __ "Got to go" warning

__ "How are you doing?"   __ Goodbyes

What I would do better next time:

Opportunity 4

I talked to:

I completed these steps during my conversation:

__ Greetings   __ "Got to go" warning

__ "How are you doing?"   __ Goodbyes

What I would do better next time:

Task 3: Parent Comments

Please comment on how your child performed when completing the conversations. Does she need more help at beginning conversations? Does she need more help at ending conversations?

Task 4: Hand in homework

Please hand in the homework to the coach at the beginning of the next social group.

Final Week Info Sheet

Next week is the final week of our social group. We are celebrating by having an outing where your child can practice their new skills in a natural environment. Here are the details.

Activity:

Drop-off Time & Place:

Pickup Time and Place:

Parent Summary Week 12

Here is a short summary of the key information your child learned during the *How to Talk with Friends* course. Use it as a reminder for what to focus on over the next few months.

Find out your friend's interests

> What is your favorite _____? e.g. What is your favorite movie?

> What did you do last _____? e.g. What did you do last weekend?

Use topic-starter questions

Used to start a conversation with a friend after greetings, or to begin a new topic during a conversation. Generally, topic-starter questions must be:

- Related to the interests of the friend, not the interests of the speaker. Shared interests are okay.
- About recent activity related to that interest

Some examples of topic-starter questions are:

> *John, did you play Minecraft this week?*

> *Megan, did you go see the Angry Birds movie like you planned?*

Comment when your friend says something

Comment when your friend does something or says something.

Match the comment to the information.

e.g. Happy comments for happy information. Sad comments for sad information.

Continue the conversation with a follow-up comment or a follow-up question

Follow-up questions ask for more information about what was just said.

Follow-up comments contain NEW information and are RELATED to what the person just said.

Pay attention to your own body language

Use your body and your eyes to show you are interested in what your friend is saying.

Pay attention to the rules for changing topics

- You have to be an active part of a conversation before you can change the topic.
- The new topic must be interesting to your friends.
- You need to wait for a gap in the conversation. This means the current topic is slowing down and everyone is ready for a new topic.

Choose appropriate topics

Filter thoughts before speaking

- You should filter a thought if you would feel bad if someone said it to you.
- You filter a thought by finding something nice to say instead.

Remember all the steps of the conversation diagram

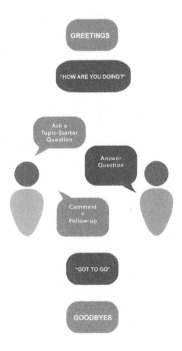

Appendix B
Weekly Materials

Appendix B contains all the worksheets and resources you need to teach each weekly lesson.

The preparation section of each lesson specifies what needs to be printed.

Week 1 Detective Notes

My Name:	Name:
Name:	**Name:**

Week 2: Game Show Questions

Here are 15 questions to ask during the Week 2 game show. While these questions are perfectly acceptable, it is even better if you also create questions relevant to the interests of your students and their family members.

These questions are in no particular order

I have an aunt who likes knitting. I haven't seen her for a few weeks. What is a good topic starter question?

I haven't seen my friend Sandra over the summer. We see each other on the first day of school. What is a good conversation starter?

My mom goes to book club once per month. What can I ask her when she gets home?

My dad plays hockey every Friday night. What can I ask him when I see him on Saturday morning?

I run into my friend Aidan at the library. I haven't seen him for a year and I can't remember what he is interested in. What can I ask after I have said "Hi" to him?

I have an uncle who likes sailing. I haven't seen him for a few weeks. What is a good topic starter question?

I have a friend who likes Pokémon Go. I haven't seen him for a few days. What is a good topic starter question?

I have a cousin who likes drawing. I haven't seen her for a few days. What is a good topic starter question?

I have an aunt who likes baking. I haven't seen her for a few weeks. What is a good topic starter question?

I have a friend who likes playing Minecraft. I haven't seen him since yesterday. What is a good topic-starter question?

My mom has just started taking an accounting course at college. What can I ask her when she gets home from class?

My aunt just arrived from Australia after a long flight. What can I ask her?

I see my best friend at school on Monday. I know he wanted to see a movie on the weekend. What topic-starter question can I ask?

My cousin just got back from a trip to Disneyland. What can I ask him?

My friend just moved into a new house on the weekend. What can I ask?

My dad just got home from grocery shopping. What topic-starter question can I ask?

One of the girls in my class has just started learning how to make jewelry. What can I ask?

My friend went shopping for a Halloween costume on the weekend. What can I ask?

My friend had cousins visiting on the weekend. What can I ask?

My sister started high school today. What can I ask her when she gets home?

Weeks 3, 4 & 5 Conversation Sentences

Print and cut the following into separate pieces so they can be picked at random from a bowl.

I went to the movies yesterday.

I saw a shooting star last night.

My dog had puppies.

We got a kitten yesterday.

My grandma is coming to visit next week.

My grandfather gave me five dollars.

I played Pokémon Go yesterday.

I built a super cool roller coaster in Minecraft.

We went to the beach.

I got to stay home from school yesterday.

My cat has to go to the vet today.

My little brother broke his arm on the jungle gym.

Our car got a flat tire on the weekend.

I crashed my bike and now it is broken.

Our cat got chased by a raccoon.

I got to eat a hot dog today.

My mom cooked macaroni and cheese last night and that's my favorite dinner.

My mom says we can get a dog.

We got a new car.

My dad is in New York.

I want a new bike for Christmas.

I tried rollerblading on the weekend. It is scary but cool.

I read books on my iPad instead of getting them from the library.

Beaches are my favorite place to play.

My aunt and uncle are coming to stay this Thanksgiving.

The rain is so hard today.

I've got 15 games for my PS4.

Mom won't let me get a mouse as a pet.

Italian food is yummy. Pizza is the best.

The library has got a lot of new books.

Comic books are awesome.

I went shopping with my mom and there are so many cool new sneakers I want.

The new French teacher is nice.

I want to be a famous singer when I grow up.

Basketball players have so much money!

Our new computer is super-fast.

I love playing Minecraft online but my dad doesn't always let me.

That thunder is scary.

My dad drives really fast on the freeway.

Disneyland is cool. I want to go.

The zoo has some awesome animals.

This Wi-Fi is really slow.

I keep forgetting my password.

My keys are gone. They must have fallen out of my pocket.

I got a new cell phone. I love it.

I don't use my iPod much now. I listen to music on my phone.

The MacBook is easy to use. I like it better than the PC.

Mom is taking us to the movies later.

I got so many Christmas presents.

This chocolate tastes great.

It's too cold in this room.

I don't like this music.

I watched baseball on TV all weekend.

I love hanging out at your house.

Your Mom is cool.

My Dad got really mad this morning.

Math is really hard.

I love playing drums in music.

The new IT teacher lets us play games for the last ten minutes.

I don't like playing tennis.

I keep playing Pokémon Go.

Your Internet is fast.

My bag is already packed for our Hawaii vacation.

Learning about other countries is interesting.

I love eating popcorn at the movies.

Our new car can go off the road.

Dogs are scary sometimes.

Those monkeys in the zoo were very smart.

It was cold when we went to Canada.

I love watching movies on the plane.

I love catching the bus.

I like doing science experiments.

We're drawing cartoons in Art today.

There won't be class if it snows tomorrow.

I left my bike lock at home.

My mom makes me wear a hat when it's sunny.

These birds are noisy.

Sharks look so dangerous.

Our new house is big.

I like riding to school more than walking.

High school looks so big and I'm worried I'll get lost.

I have nearly all the cars in Asphalt 8 now. It's my favorite game.

I have 5 dollars. I don't know whether to get candy or chocolate.

The new school lunches taste great.

Flying can be boring but planes are cool.

I have so many new clothes I don't know what to wear.

Your sister annoys me.

These seats are uncomfortable.

The food on the airplane tastes weird.

I wish my parents gave me as much pocket money as you get!

I'm thinking of doing a paper route next year.

I want to be a movie star.

Sports Day is so cool.

Week 5 Conversation Questions

Print and cut the following into separate pieces so they can be picked at random from a bowl.

What did you do on the weekend?

Have you played any good video games lately?

Did you finish your math homework?

Do you like funny shows?

Have you seen the movie Finding Dory?

Do you like playing baseball?

Did you watch TV last night?

Have you got any pets?

Have you got any brothers or sisters?

Have you been to a live sports game?

Where did you get your T-shirt?

Do you like pizza?

Do you like your teacher?

Do you like pop music?

What's your favorite class at school?

Who is your best friend?

Have you been on a roller coaster?

Did you watch a movie last night?

Where do you eat lunch?

Have you been to France?

Do you like pasta?

Have you ever been in a Christmas concert?

How do you get to school in the morning?

Are you going on vacation this summer?

Have you got a bike?

Do you play tennis?

Are you good at video games?

What sports do you play?

What is your favorite video game?

Week 6 Conversation Topics

Video games

Soccer

Hockey

Food

Italian food

iPad

Apps

X-Box / Wii U / Play Station

Laptop computers

Favorite TV shows

Favorite music

Bikes

Favorite sport

Cars

Places to travel

Most fun vacation

Pets

Animals

School

Thunderstorms

Snow storms

My family

My friends

Favorite singer

My parents

My brothers and sisters

My favorite movies

Pokémon Go

Minecraft

Pizza

Pasta

Soda / Pop

Ice cream

Asphalt 8

Mario Kart

Miami Heat

Favorite sports team

Android phones or iPhones

Math tests

Harry Potter

Favorite ride at a theme park

Visiting the zoo

Skiing

Snowboarding

Skateboarding

Plans for this weekend

Favorite teacher

Favorite hobby

Week 6 Conversation Parts

Print and cut the following into separate pieces so they can be picked at random from a bowl.

Topic-starter Question

Short Comment

Follow-up Comment

Follow-up Question

Week 7 Conversation Clues & Questions

Question #1

What level are you up to in Geometry Dash?

Question #2

What sights did you see in Seattle when you visited?

Conversation Clues

I didn't go to the movies this weekend. I went bike riding.

I don't like Mario Kart. I prefer Skylanders.

Did you see that show on TV about earthquakes?

Have you ever seen a whale? I saw one on the weekend.

Our math teacher is so unfair!

My mom drives me crazy.

Have you played Roboblox? It's awesome.

--- for more ideas, see the Week 3,4,5 Conversation Sentences. Most will apply here, too. ---

Week 7 Game Show Questions

A: What did you do on the weekend?

B: I am going to California next weekend.

A: What did you do on the weekend?

B: I went surfing at the beach.

A: I don't watch Monster High anymore.

B: Who is your favorite character?

A: I don't watch Monster High anymore.

B: Are you watching anything new?

A: I hate school!

B: Who is your favorite teacher?

A: I hate school!

B: How come?

A: I went to the amusement park on Sunday.

B: Did you have a hot dog for lunch?

A: I went to the amusement park on Sunday.

B: What rides did you go on?

A: Did you enjoy karate class?

B: I went to the coffee shop afterwards.

A: Did you enjoy karate class?

B: Yes, I am nearly ready to test for my next belt.

A: What grade are you in this year?

B: My teacher drinks pop every day.

A: What grade are you in this year?

B: I'm in grade 5. My teacher is Mr Meyers.

A: Can you tell me how to pass this level?

B: I passed that easily.

A: Can you tell me how to pass this level?

B: Sure. You need to jump just before the tunnel.

A: Where did you get your shoes?

B: I don't know. My mom got them.

A: Where did you get your shoes?

B: My shirt is new.

Week 10 Filter Scenarios

Print and cut the following examples into separate pieces so they can be picked at random from a bowl.

No filter needed:

Your friend arrives at school with a cool new backpack. She shows it to you proudly. You think it is awesome.

It's the start of the winter vacation. Your Mom comes home and tells you that you will all be going skiing next week. You are incredibly excited.

You watch your friend win at tennis. Afterward she asks you how she played. You think she was really good.

You walk into the den and see a large new TV. You are so happy! You run off to see your mom.

Your uncle gives you 10 dollars. You are excited.

You get a new MacBook for Christmas. You love it!

Your Mom asks you what you think of dinner. It's your favorite meal.

You have an important football match but there's a storm. You're really disappointed.

Your friend arrives with his Dad in a cool new convertible car. He asks you what you think of it. You think it is really cool.

You come first in the English quiz. You're very proud and happy. Your teacher asks you how you feel.

Need to filter:

You are about to watch your favorite TV show, but your grandma arrives for a visit. Now you have to sit and talk to her. You are pretty mad about this and you wish she would go home.

Your friend asks you what you think of her new haircut. You don't like it.

Your friend asks you to return the pen he lent you. You can't find it.

Your Dad asks what you think of his new jeans. You don't like them.

Your cousin asks if you think the way your uncle dresses makes him look old-fashioned. You think he does look old-fashioned.

Your friend asks if you find his grandfather scary. He says strange things and you do find him a bit scary. You don't want to upset your friend.

Your best friend asks if you think her Mom is too old to have her hair dyed pink. You think she is too old.

Your grandmother asks if you liked the Christmas present she got you last year. You didn't like it much.

Your friend asks if you find his Dad embarrassing because he laughs so loudly and tells silly jokes. You do think your friend's dad is embarrassing.

Your friend has to go to bed at 7:00. She asks if you think this is too early. You do think it is early.

Your Nan cooked you dinner and asks if you liked the meal. The gravy was lumpy and you hate carrots.

Your Grandfather makes you a hot chocolate but you only like cold drinks. He asks how you like it.

Your cousin asks if you like your aunt playing the piano. She is very good but you don't like that kind of music.

Every time you visit your grandparents they always want to play a card game you don't enjoy after dinner. Once again, they ask if you want to play cards with them.

Your brother asks if you want the last piece of pizza or if he can have it. You are still hungry and it's your favorite kind.

Your grandmother has her music on and you don't like it at all. She asks if you like the music.

Your Mom asks if you want to visit your great aunt. You find it very boring at her house. You just have to sit there and watch TV while she and your Mom chat.

Your grandfather starts telling you a joke he has told you already. He asks you if he has told you this one before.

Your uncle asks if you mind if he smokes. You hate the smell of cigarettes.

Your grandmother's neighbor offers you a coat which he thought you might like. It doesn't look like it would fit and you don't like it.

Your Chinese friend asks you to have dinner with his family. You can't use chopsticks and you worry you might look silly.

Your friend asks you to come for a sleep over. You are still scared of the dark! You worry about being in the dark even with your friend there.

A boy in class tries to get you to say something mean. You don't want to.

Your uncle loves his new car. He asks what you think. You think the car is ugly.

Appendix C
Assessment Sheets

In this section you will find the assessment sheets that the coach uses during each weekly session. Only one assessment sheet is needed for up to four students.

Most assessment activities specify a required target behavior and the coach scores each student as follows.

++ Mostly without prompting

Use this code if your student performs the required task without prompting, or occasionally needs a gestural or visual prompt.

+ Mostly with minor prompting

Use this code if your student often needs gestural or visual prompts and occasionally needs full or partial verbal prompts.

- Mostly with extensive prompting

Use this code if your student often needs partial or full verbal prompts.

N/A

Use this code if the student did not have the opportunity to achieve the specified task during the activity.

Assessment Week 1

++ Mostly without prompting   + Mostly minor prompting   – Mostly extensive prompting

Detective Practice Activity

Student Name				
Used 'Favorite' Question				
Used 'What did you do' Question				

Snack

Student Name				
Asked a question				
Responded to a question				

Board Game

Student Name				
Participated in game				
Asked a question				
Responded to a question				

Game Show

Student Name				
Participated				
Mostly answered questions correctly				

Group Activity

Student Name				
Participated				
Asked a question				
Responded to a question				

Additional Notes:

Assessment Week 2

++ Mostly without prompting   + Mostly minor prompting   – Mostly extensive prompting

Practice Activity

Student Name				
Asked appropriate topic-starter question				
Answered topic-starter question appropriately.				

Snack

Student Name				
Asked appropriate topic-starter question				
Answered topic-starter question appropriately.				

Board Game

Student Name				
Participated in game				
Asked appropriate topic-starter question				
Answered topic-starter question appropriately.				

Game Show

Student Name				
Participated				
Mostly answered questions correctly				

Group Activity

Student Name				
Participated				
Asked appropriate topic-starter question				
Answered topic-starter question appropriately.				

Additional Notes:

Assessment Week 3

++ Mostly without prompting   + Mostly minor prompting   – Mostly extensive prompting

Practice Activity

Student Name				
Made appropriate comments				

Snack

Student Name				
Made appropriate comments				

Board Game

Student Name				
Participated in game				
Made appropriate comments				

Game Show

Student Name				
Participated				
Made appropriate comments				

Group Activity

Student Name				
Participated				
Made appropriate comments				

Additional Notes:

Assessment Week 4

++ Mostly without prompting   + Mostly minor prompting   – Mostly extensive prompting

Practice Activity

Student Name				
Made appropriate follow-up questions				

Snack

Student Name				
Made appropriate follow-up questions				

Board Game

Student Name				
Participated in game				
Made appropriate follow-up questions				

Game Show

Student Name				
Participated				
Made appropriate follow-up questions				

Group Activity

Student Name				
Participated				
Made appropriate follow-up questions				

Additional Notes:

Assessment Week 5

++ Mostly without prompting   + Mostly minor prompting   – Mostly extensive prompting

Practice Activity

Student Name				
Made appropriate follow-up comments				

Snack

Student Name				
Made appropriate conversation				

Board Game

Student Name				
Participated in game				
Made appropriate conversation				

Game Show

Student Name				
Participated				
Made appropriate follow-up comments				

Group Activity

Student Name				
Participated				
Made appropriate conversation				

Additional Notes:

Assessment Week 6

++ Mostly without prompting   + Mostly minor prompting   − Mostly extensive prompting

Practice Activity

Student Name				
Made appropriate conversation				

Snack

Student Name				
Made appropriate conversation				

Board Game

Student Name				
Participated in game				
Made appropriate conversation				

Game Show

Student Name				
Participated				
Made appropriate answers				

Group Activity

Student Name				
Participated				
Made appropriate conversation				

Additional Notes:

Assessment Week 7

++ Mostly without prompting   + Mostly minor prompting   – Mostly extensive prompting

Practice Activity

Student Name				
Followed topic changes				
Avoided special interest				

Snack

Student Name				
Followed topic changes				
Avoided special interest				

Board Game

Student Name				
Followed topic changes				
Avoided special interest				

Game Show

Student Name				
Participated				

Group Activity

Student Name				
Followed topic changes				
Avoided special interest				

Additional Notes:

Assessment Week 8

++ Mostly without prompting   + Mostly minor prompting   − Mostly extensive prompting

Practice Activity

Student Name				
Participated before changing topic				
Chose good gap for topic change				

Snack

Student Name				
Participated before changing topic				
Chose good topic				
Chose good gap for topic change				

Board Game

Student Name				
Participated before changing topic				
Chose good topic				
Chose good gap for topic change				

Game Show

Student Name				
Participated				
Skill improvement				

Group Activity

Student Name				
Participated before changing topic				
Chose good topic				
Chose good gap for topic change				

Additional Notes:

Assessment Week 9

++ Mostly without prompting   + Mostly minor prompting   − Mostly extensive prompting

Practice Activity

Student Name				
Demonstrated appropriate body language				

Snack

Student Name				
Demonstrated appropriate body language				

Board Game

Student Name				
Participated in game				
Demonstrated appropriate body language				

Game Show

Student Name				
Participated				
Demonstrated appropriate body language				

Group Activity

Student Name				
Participated				
Demonstrated appropriate body language				

Additional Notes:

Assessment Week 10

++ Mostly without prompting   + Mostly minor prompting   – Mostly extensive prompting

Practice Activity

Student Name				
Filtered appropriately				

Snack

Student Name				
Made appropriate conversation				

Board Game

Student Name				
Participated in game				
Made appropriate conversation				
Filtered appropriately				

Game Show

Student Name				
Participated				
Filtered appropriately				

Group Activity

Student Name				
Participated				
Made appropriate conversation				
Filtered appropriately				

Additional Notes:

Assessment Week 11

++ Mostly without prompting   + Mostly minor prompting   – Mostly extensive prompting

Practice Activity

Student Name				
Successfully began and warmed up conversation				
Successfully cooled and completed conversation				

Snack

Student Name				
Participated in conversation				
Appropriate questions and comments				

Board Game

Student Name				
Participated in conversation				
Appropriate questions and comments				

Game Show

Student Name				
Participated				

Group Activity

Student Name				
Appropriate answers				

Additional Notes:

Assessment Week 12

Student 1:

Student Name	
Biggest Improvement	
Biggest Challenge	
Specific Suggestion for Parents	

Student 2:

Student Name	
Biggest Improvement	
Biggest Challenge	
Specific Suggestion for Parents	

Student 3:

Student Name	
Biggest Improvement	
Biggest Challenge	
Specific Suggestion for Parents	

Student 4:

Student Name	
Biggest Improvement	
Biggest Challenge	
Specific Suggestion for Parents	

Appendix D
Signs & Images

In this appendix you will find the images and signs mentioned in the weekly lessons.

The images are used in the social skills lesson. Images included are:

- Conversation diagrams
- Active brain image

The signs are used as visual prompts as specified in each lesson. Most signs are used across multiple weeks, so keep them once you have printed them. Laminating can also be handy.

Signs included are:

- Ask a Topic-starter Question
- Comment
- Comment + Follow-up Question
- Follow-up Comment or Question
- Too Long
- Keep Talking

A blank certificate of achievement is also included for your use.

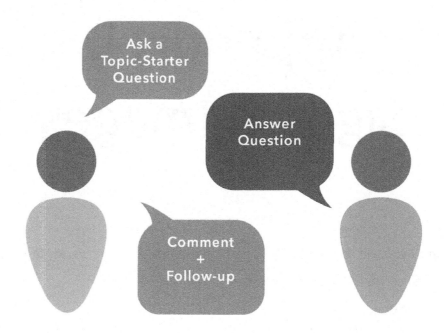

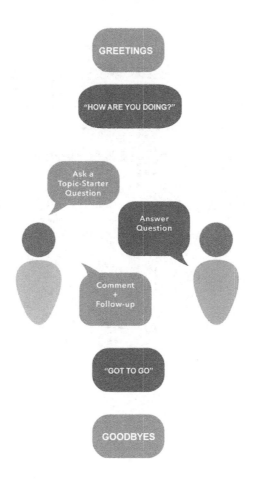

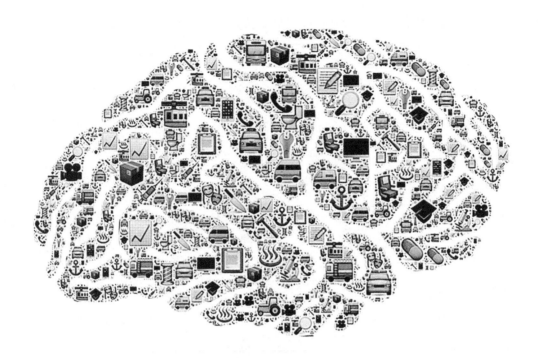

Ask a Topic-starter Question

Comment

Comment

+

Follow-up

Follow-up Comment
or
Follow-up Question

Keep Talking

CERTIFICATE
OF
ACHIEVEMENT

THIS CERTIFICATE IS AWARDED TO

_____

IN RECOGNITION OF

_____

_____   _____
DATE   **SIGNATURE**

Can You Help...?

Happy Frog Press is a small high-quality press providing much-needed resources to families and professionals working with children with Autism and other social/language challenges.

Your help in leaving a positive review on Amazon makes a HUGE difference for us. And you can leave a review on Amazon even if you purchased the book somewhere else.

If you have found value in this book, please go to Amazon.com (or your local equivalent) and search for 'social skills curriculum.' Select our book and scroll down to the reviews. You will see an 'Add a review' button.

If you received the book as a promotion, Amazon requires you to acknowledge that.

We thank you for your support!

If you do leave us a review, let us know via our website www.HappyFrogApps.com so we can thank you in person. We also have free downloads to make delivering this course even easier!

Need More Resources?

Happy Frog Apps and Happy Frog Press create quality resources for elementary-aged children with autism and other social/language challenges.

Our award-winning apps target reading comprehension, vocabulary and math skills at the Grade 2–4 level.

Our users love the built-in rewards and carefully graduated incremental learning.

SLPs, teachers and parents love the detailed reporting and success-driven design.

Visit our website today to sign up for FREE apps!

www.Facebook.com/HappyFrogApps

@HappyFrogApps

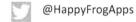

www.HappyFrogApps.com

75367080R00155